THE ROAD & THE STREET

The Story of the Boy who Couldn't Whistle

Jeff Brent

Dedicated to Mother Earth

The Road & The Street
The Story of the Boy Who Couldn't Whistle
By Jeff Brent

ISBN-13: 9798517189554

copyright © 2021

front cover artwork: Jesus Aguayo

intro

Mom always told me, *"Leave this world a better place than what you found it."* I also took that to mean *make it a better place <u>during</u> my time here too.*

I did everything that I could do, and I saw everything that I could see.

I experienced civilization and culture on this orb as only a human being can. I traveled as a participant, not a spectator, on my voyage through this life.

You might wonder, *"Why did you even write this, Jeff?"*

I *didn't* write it – It wrote itself. I didn't even have to think up stuff. The stories were already there. All I had to do was re-experience things as they happened and document it. Just a walk down the garden path.

This is not fiction. I honestly haven't had to invent or exaggerate anything, the events all occurred as described.

How did *I* make things better? For one thing, playing music for all kinds of parties, concerts, and festivals, you name it. Yes, that *does* make this planet a better place.

Teaching language and showing people how to play instruments makes the world better, too. My many published books add significantly to the sum of human knowledge.

I see these as my major accomplishments:

- Solved the riddle of why, in music, a root's strongest pull is up a 4th. This is the $E=mc^2$ of harmonic motion in tonal musics. Never been done before.

- Revolutionized music theory by discovering that the structure of the pentatonic and major scales, etc are derived radiating symmetrically from a central axis. Never before seen.

- Invented a new music notation system via a graphic form of representation that can be read by trained musicians, yet flexible enough to represent all sonic phenomena (bird calls, whale songs, Silbo Gomero, etc). And it's pretty too.

- Reconciled Evolution and Creation. Those who came before are within us now. The human race is one grand continuous organism progressing towards making a better world for all people and maintaining the ecological health of our tiny blue home.

~ the meaning of life is to create ~

Table of Contents

THE ROAD (part one)

<u>Welcome</u>	1
city	4
dent	6
primate	8
hedge	8
<u>Brother</u>	10
invulnerable	11
crows	11
sitters	13
echo	14
read	16
mob	16
balloon	18
garden	18
firsts	19
<u>Sister</u>	21
toad	22
movies	24
<u>second</u>	25
<u>third</u>	26
Noble	27
burma	28
liberty	29
bees	29
slow	29
<u>4.1</u>	31
<u>4.2</u>	32
guts	33
fort	36
cox	37
toro	40
chupacabra	42
<u>fifth</u>	43
strider	44
clam	52
<u>sixth</u>	53
crystal	53
shoulders	54
surf	60
love	62
Frank	63
grapefruit	67
<u>seventh</u>	69
chuzya	70
sic	71
halloween	72
goober	72
imprint	74
candy	78
<u>8.2</u>	85
fish	85
Corbetta	87
<u>ninth</u>	88
freaks	90
mystic	90
1969	92
girlfriend	93
choice	95
woodsie	95
<u>tenth</u>	100
ruby	100
n^2o	100
gtr	101
alfalfa	101
lottery	103
C7	104
unfired	106
fur	106
<u>eleventh</u>	108
Noble	109
man	109
sylmar	116
toast	116
beat	118
Guinevere	120
bread	127
schaum	129
matters	129
boar	130
cheat	130
<u>twelfth</u>	134
truckin'	135
swing	136
schmuck	139
graduation	140

<u>college</u>	140
wizard	141
crumb	143
toots	144
thumbs	147
knight	151
purée	153
simulcasts	154
ménage	155
<u>1973</u>	162
breakfast	164
nevermore	166
board	168
thirtysex	169
fountain	172
skool	176
<u>1974</u>	176
Jessi	178
knocks	179
etiquette	181
child	182
instruction	183
canyon	187
<u>1975</u>	191
thunderbird	192
broke	194
university	196
ragtime	198
phone	200
nye	202
pdq	204
heart	205
mathamphetamine	208
theory	209
<u>twenty-one</u>	212
Portland	213
WV	216
saltimbocca	219
pigtown	222
birthday	224
sand	226
strippers	227
blastoff	229
Europe	232
Dieu	232
sud	234
comics	235
wall	235
Tréguier	236
Brighton	240
Scotland	242
bartender	243
passport stamps	245
THE STREET	253
Foreword	254
Mr Ax	259
Nurf Twins	263
Loony Burg	264
TooRich Zürich	266
Sperlonga	277
Cidalia	280
Dolly & her Doggy	284
Alice	288
Cologne	311
Ireland	315
Ten Franc Piece	320
The Week	324
Les Artistes	332
Vienna Dee	340
Just a Minute	348
A Pitch in Munich	358
Magic Carpet Ride	361
Samantha	363
Polo & Hanery	366
Hannover	374
Ahoy	378
Wakes	387
-30-	398

Appendix 399

languages
Français	400
Deutsch	401
Schviizertuutsch	401
Español	402
Italiano	403
Silbo Gomero	405
العربية	406
Português	407
Nederlands	408
Esperanto	408
Русский	410
हिंदी	411
اردو	411
Ελληνικά	412

recordings
mp3s & midi	413
videos	419

bibliography
music theory books	420
music technique books	421

literature I've read
classics	424
religion	426

my resumé 3/2020 — 427
published music books	428
formal education	428
teaching experience	429
performance experience	429
instruments & styles	429
artists studied	429
further music education	430
current projects	431
websites	431
discography & video	432
life experience	432
languages	432

Other writings
lyrics
Allusion	433
Third Circle	433
Gypsy Lullaby	434
¿How Come?	434
Mackie's Back	435
Fox in Hen House	435
Honky Tonk Bars	437
Dodge	438
Dyin' Inside	439
Marilyn	440
Truck Stop	441
Good Business	442
From Time to Time	443
Your Heat	444
Moonshine Run	445
I Need Love	446
The Reason Why	446
Louisiana Calling	447
Calico Lady	448
Time Moves Along	448
Chuggaluggin'	449
Mainstream	450
Ditty Daw	451
Wedja Sedja Bin	452
Leaf Upon the Wind	452
Nothing Else	453
Sunset Worlds	454
One-Eyed Jacks	455
Coins of Stone	456
Seven Days of Rain	456
What You Need	457
Down to the Sun	458
Escape from the Past	458
Chopped Liver Blues	459
Maureen Marine	460

poetry & prose
Nothing	463
Absinthe	463
The Wedding Poem	464
Rogaine	464
Next to the River	464
Limelight	465
Long Time Ago	465
The Brink	466
Zone Dog	466
The Border	467
Untitled	467
Friday's Child	467

Welcome

Here I am at my parents' wedding. They both just graduated high school. My mom is a few days shy of her eighteenth birthday, and my dad will still be 17 for another few months.

I'm not showing yet in the above pic, but this is how I appeared about eight months later.

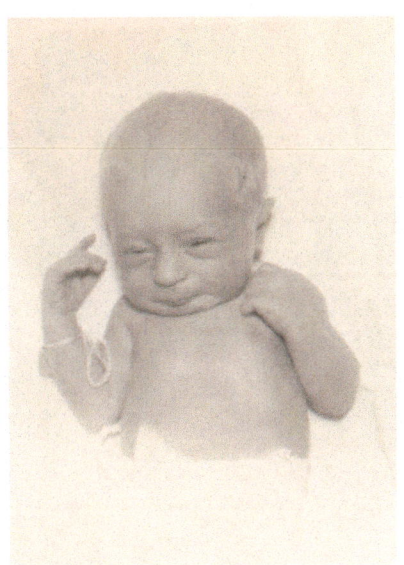

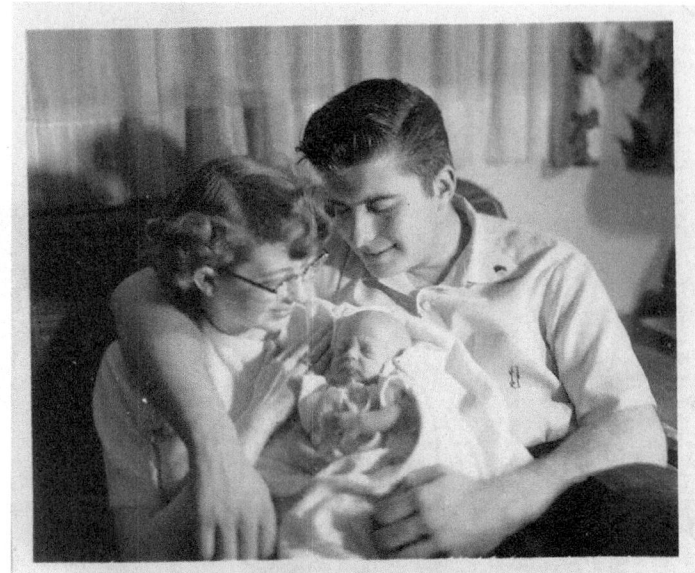
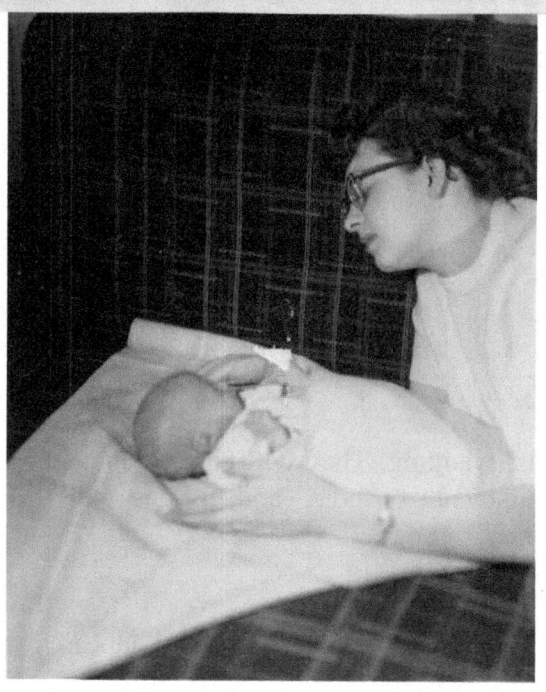
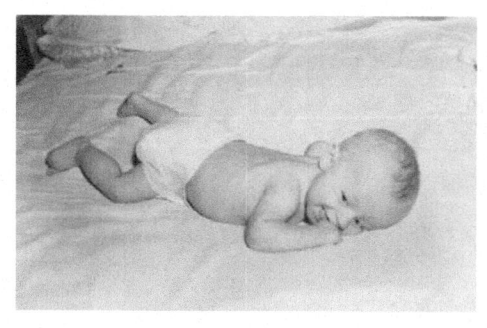
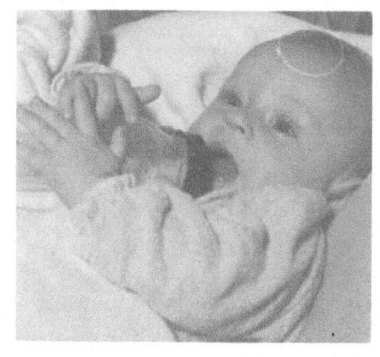

Gospel Songs

Peace Like a River	p. 125
This Little Light of Mine	p. 126
Amazing Grace	p. 127
We Shall Overcome	p. 128
Study War No More	p. 129
Go Down, Moses	p. 130
Let Your Light Shine On Me	p. 131
Kum Ba Yah	p. 132
I'll Fly Away	p. 133
Glory Glory Hallelujah	p. 134
Rise and Shine	p. 135
When the Saints Go Marchin' In.	p. 136
The Glory Train	p. 137
The Lion of Judah	p. 139
And We Bid You Goodnite	p. 141

Folk Songs

This Land is Your Land	p. 144
Guantanamera	p. 145
Blowin' in the Wind	p. 146
Turn! Turn! Turn!	p. 147
Hava Nagilah	p. 148
Paranue	p. 149
Ushavtem Mayim	p. 150
The Water Is Wide	p. 151

Devotional Songs

I Am As God Created Me	p. 154
The Prayer of Saint Francis.	p. 155
Love, Serve, Remember	p. 156
Gesher Tsar Me'od	p. 157
Only Here for Love	p. 158
The Greatest Commandment	p. 159
Hinei Ma Tov	p. 160
Little Drummer Boy	p. 161
Hodu L'Adonai	p. 163
Simple Gifts	p. 164
E'Malama	p. 165
Walk In Beauty	p. 166
How Could Anyone?	p. 168
La Promesa	p. 169
Altar of Love	p. 170
We All Come from the Goddess	p. 171
Ode to Joy	p. 173
Forever We Are	p. 175
Ani Ve'Ata	p. 177

Children's Songs

Every Little Cell	p. 181
I've Been Working on the Railroad	p. 183
Twinkle Twinkle Little Star	p. 184
Awaken, Children	p. 186
Row Row Row Your Boat	p. 187
Yes, We Have No Bananas	p. 189
When We Were Living in Caves	p. 191
Cottlestone Pie	p. 192
Frere Jacques	p. 193
Hawaiian Rainbows	p. 194
Tap Tap Tapusky	p. 195
Happy Birthday to You	p. 196
Happy, Happy Birthday!	p. 197
We Vishnu a Hare Krishna	p. 198
Dobru Noc	p. 199

Our Songs

In My Book.	p. 205
Into Her Presence	p. 210
Here We are	p. 212
The Forgotten Song	p. 214
The Wings of Song	p. 215
Rock Steady	p. 216
All Are Called	p. 217
Heart 'n' Hands	p. 218

Let's Get Hitched	**p. 219**
The Music Now	**p. 220**
I Am Spirit	**p. 221**
I Believe in Miracles	**p. 222**
The Peace of God is Shining	**p. 224**
Love Is Letting Go	**p. 226**
Losin' the Illusion	**p. 227**
Clear As Morning	**p. 228**
Good Cheer	**p. 229**
US Anthem	**p. 230**
Holy Encounter	**p. 232**
Are You Coming?	**p. 233**
Light of the World	**p. 234**
Love Won	**p. 235**
My Religion	**p. 236**
Christmas Presence	**p. 237**
Be Still	**p. 238**
One Life	**p. 239**
The Attitude of Gratitude	**p. 240**
The Risen Sun	**p. 242**
God Is	**p. 243**
Live on Love	**p. 244**
Walk in Glory	**p. 246**
Don't Worry, Be Happy	**p. 248**
Forgiveness Sets Us Free	**p. 250**
Holy Mother Full of Grace	**p. 252**
Fight in the Dog	**p. 253**

'Til the Break of Day	p. 254
Return to the Garden of Love	p. 255
I Will Be Still a Moment	p. 256
Everyone Knows What Love Is	p. 257
Truly Helpful	p. 258
So Long	p. 259
Bless You, Brother	p. 260
Love Is Here	p. 261
State of Grace	p. 262
Ready for Love	p. 263
How Lovely	p. 265
Happy Unbirthday to Me	p. 266
For the Love of God	p. 267
Song of a Sunflower	p. 269
Stay Wild	p. 270
Let It Be Undone	p. 271
Sunsmile	p. 272
Come Home	p. 273
One Dance	p. 275
To Change the World	p. 277
Jah Makeah, No Problem	p. 279
Choose Once Again	p. 282
Rejoicing	p. 284
Your Grace is Given Me	p. 285
Happy Song	p. 287
Breathe	p. 288
The Greeting	p. 289

When Will There Be
   Peace on Earth?   p. 290

Poems

Look to This Day	p. 293
Wean Yourself	p. 294
Awake to the Name	p. 295
Quest for God	p. 297
Take Peace, Take Heaven	p. 299
Simply Do This	p. 300
Tomorrow Never Knows	p. 301
Brahman	p. 303
The Invitation	p. 305
Akla Cholo Re	p. 308
The Way of the Warrior	p. 309
God Is	p. 312
The Beatitudes	p. 314
Samadhi	p. 315
Nirvana	p. 317
The Master's Prayer	p. 319
To Everything There Is a Season.	p. 322
Judge Not Yourself	p. 324
Nirvana-Shatakam	p. 325
Yoga Means Union	p. 330
I Follow the Religion of Love	p. 331
Beyond the Body	p. 332

She Let Go	**p. 333**
As I Began to Love Myself	**p. 335**
Love	**p. 337**
Sri Atma Gita	**p. 339**
The Inner Ruler	**p. 347**
The Music Cannot Be Written	**p. 349**
The Highest Bliss	**p. 351**
Love Never Fails	**p. 353**
On Love	**p. 355**

MANTRAS & KIRTAN

Kirtan

Kirtan is part of the Bhakti Yoga path,
also known as the Devotional Path of yoga.
The practice traditionally involves call-and-response singing
of sacred names in a group
generally using instruments like the harmonium
(brought to India by the British), guitar, percussion, tablas, bells, etc.
It's all to bring you more into a devotional heartspace,

where the ego-mind dissolves

and there is a feeling of love and oneness.

It's been really catching on in the West in the past 3 decades or so,

and especially in the past 10 years,

so much that there are even kirtan festivals now.

I personally feel that kirtan can be a deeper and more fulfilling practice

than mere asana, but even more potent when combined!

KEY

Jai or **Jaya** means "Yay!" or "Victory!"

Namah = Bow to, Pay Homage to

Shanti = Peace

OM or **AUM** starts almost every mantra

Bolo = Sing!

Bhajan = Devotional Song

OM is the Word

Chords: A D G

3~'

AUM is the primordial sound, the Cosmic Hum,
the sound of God, Yes!

Omkaram Bindu Samyuktam
Nityam Dhyayanti Yoginaha
Kamadam Mokshadam Chaiva
Omkaraaaya Namo Namaha
Omkaraaya Namo Namaha

OM is the Word
Ohhhh hmmm? Have you heard?...
Ommmm can take you home
Ohhhh Om Sweet Om

3~'

Saha Navavatu Mantra

Om Saha Navavatu
Saha Nau Bhunaktu
Saha Viiryam Karavaavahai
Tejasvi Nau-Adhii-Tam-Astu
Maa Vidvishaavahai
Om Shaantih Shaantih Shaantihi

May God protect us both
(the teacher and the student).

May we work together with
energy and vigor.

May our study be enlightening,
not giving rise to hostility.

Om peace peace peace

om saha nāvavatu
saha nau bhunaktu
saha vīryaṁ karavāvahai
tejasvi nāvadhītamastu mā vidviṣāvahai
om śāntiḥ śāntiḥ śāntiḥ

ॐ सह नाववतु ।
सह नौ भुनक्तु ।
सह वीर्यं करवावहै ।
तेजस्वि नावधीतमस्तु मा विद्विषावहै ।
ॐ शान्तिः शान्तिः शान्तिः ॥

May God protect us both together,
May God nourish us together,
May we gain energy to know the Truth,
May our study together be filled with light,
May we not oppose each other.
Om Peace, Peace, Peace.

om: sacred syllable often at the commencement of prayers
saha: together with, along with
nāvavatu: may one protect
nau: both
bhunaktu: may one nourish
vīrya: strength, power, energy
karavāvahai: work or act together
tejasvi: one possessing brilliance or vigour
adhīte: to study
astu: let it be
mā: not
vidviṣ: dislike or hostility towards one another
om śāntiḥ: closing blessing bestowing peace

The Gayatri Mantra

ॐ ॐ ॐ

ॐ भूर् भुवः स्वः

तत् सवितुर्वरेण्यं

भर्गो देवस्य धीमहि

धियो यो नः प्रचोदयात्

AUM BHUR BHUVAH SVAHA

TAT SAVITUR VARENYAM

BHARGO DEVASYA DHEEMAHI

DHIYO YO NAH PRACHODAYAAT

We Meditate on the Sublime

Light of the Sun, Light of the One

May That Light Illuminate Our Minds

& May We All Live in Love!

Gayatri Mantra

ॐ भूर्भुवः स्वः, तत्सवितुर्वरेण्यं।
भर्गोदेवस्य धीमहि, धियो यो नः प्रचोदयात्।

Om Bhur-Bhuvah-Svah, Tat-Savitur-Varenyam,
Bhargo-Devasya-Dheemahi, Dhiyo-Yo-Nah-Prachodayaata.

Ganesha Song

Gam Ganapataye Namo Namah
(mantra to Ganesha)

Loka Samasta Sukhinoh Bhavantu

May Everyone Everywhere Be Happy & Free!

OM Shanti Shanti Shanti OM
May peace prevail everywhere –
Within, without & all around

Ganesha Sharanam

Ganesha sharanam sharanam Ganesha

Ganesha sharanam sharanam Ganesha

Ganesha sharanam sharanam Ganesha

Ganesha sharanam sharanam Ganesha

I take refuge in Ganesha,
Who stands at the gate
Ready to remove all obstacles in the way
of our progress to the light

OM Namah Shivaya

Om Namah Shivaya

Om Namah Shivaya

Om Namah Shivaya

Shivaya Namah OM

JAYA JAYA Shiva Shambho
JAYA JAYA Shiva Shambho

Mahadeva Shambho, Mahadeva Shambho

I bow to Śiva, the Auspicious One,
the Great God who is the Lord of Yoga,
and is another name for the guru, the master teacher,
who resides within me and all of us.

Asatoma Mantra

**Om asatoma sadgamaya/
tamasoma jyotirgamaya/
mrtyorma amrtamgamaya
om shanti shanti shantihi**

May we be led from untruth to truth
May we be led from darkness to light
May we be led from death to eternal life
Om Peace Peace Peace!

Or

May we be led to Truth from the lie
May we be led from darkness to the light
& May we be led from Death to
Immortal Life
& May we all know peace

Suddhossi Buddhossi

A Sanskrit mantra originally sung as a lullaby by a woman saint to her children in the Vedas

[Sanskrit]	[English]	[Español]
Suddhossi buddhossi niranjanosi	*You are forever pure, you are forever true*	*Tu eres siempre puro*
Samsara maya parivar jitosi	*& the dream of this world can never touch you*	*Eres verdadero*
Samsara svapanam	*So give up your attachment &*	*Y el sueño del mundo*
Traija mohan nidram	*give up your confusion*	*Nunca te tocará*
Na janma mrityor	*& fly to that space that's beyond all illusion*	*Deja los apegos*
Tat sat sva rupe		*Deja la confusion*
		Y vuela mas alla
		De toda illusion

Heart Sutra
Prajnaparamita

gate gate

pāragate

pārasaṃgate

bodhi svāhā

Gone Gone

Gone Beyond

Gone Beyond

The Great Beyond

Into The Essence

Back to the Arms of God

Into the Presence

Back to the Heart of All

AUM Shree Ram Jai Ram Jai Jai Ram!

हरे कृष्ण हरे कृष्ण
कृष्ण कृष्ण हरे हरे
हरे राम हरे राम
राम राम हरे हरे

Hare Krishna
Hare Krishna
Krishna Krishna
Hare Hare
Hare Rama
Hare Rama
Rama Rama
Hare Hare

Maha Mantra

Hare Krishna
Hare Krishna
Krishna Krishna
Hare Hare

Hare Rama
Hare Rama
Rama Rama
Hare Hare

Hare means "Lord"
It could also mean "Hooray!"

Krishna and Rama are the 2 most
well-known and loved incarnations of Vishnu,
the Preserver and Maintainer of Dharma.

This mantra is sometimes referred to as the Hare Krishna mantra,
and it's also called the "Maha Mantra," the Great Mantra.

I have heard "Hare" (pronounced "Har-ey") translated variously as
"Lord,"
"Hail," and as an epithet (name) of Vishnu.

I'll Just Be Me

Nowhere to go
Nothin' to do
No one to be
I'll just be me,
you just be you

Hare Krishna Hare Krishna
Krishna Krishna Hare Hare

Hare Rama Hare Rama
Rama Rama Hare Hare

I have no name
I have no shame
All praise & blame
It's all a game,
& It's all the same

Hare Krishna Hare Krishna
Krishna Krishna Hare Hare

Hare Rama Hare Rama
Rama Rama Hare Hare

Make up your bed
Make up your mind
Make up, you've read,
to make up is kind

'Cause It's all for free
It's all for love
It's all a dream,
& you made it up

Hare Krishna Hare Krishna
Krishna Krishna Hare Hare

Hare Rama Hare Rama
Rama Rama Hare Hare

Devakinandana Gopala

D A G D

Sri Krishna Govinda
Hare Murare
Hai Natha Narayana Vasudeva
Hai Natha Narayana Vasudeva
Hai Natha Narayana Vasudeva

Gopala Gopala
Devakinandana Gopala!

Devikananda Gopala
Devikanandana Gopala!

All Praise to Krishna,

the Protector of the Cows

& the son of Devaki

So Ham, Ham Saha

C G F C

So Ham
Ham Saha
So Ham
Ham Saha

I Am That
That I Am
I Am That
That I Am

So Ham, Ham Saha…

I Am Love
Love I Am
I Am Love
Love I Am

Eheye Asher Eheye

& Still

A7 -> Esus4
So Ham (8x)

Radhe Krishna
Radhe Krishna
Krishna Krishna
Radhe Radhe

Radhe Shyama
Radhe Shyama
Shyama Shyama
Radhe Radhe

& Still
& Still
& Still I love you
& Still I love you
& Still I love you
& Still

So Ham
So Ham
So Ham

Baba Hanuman

```
C    F C    F C       F    C        F
Namo... Namo...   Anjaninandanaaya
```

```
      C                        F
Jaya Seeyaa Raama, Jai Jai Hanumaan
      C                        F
Jaya Seeyaa Raama, Jai Jai Hanumaan
       Dm                      F
Jaya Seeyaa Raama, Jai Jai Hanumaan
       Dm                      F
Jaya Seeyaa Raama, Jai Jai Hanumaan
```

```
        C                  F
Jaya Bajrangbalee,   Baba Hanuman
        C                  F
Jaya Bajrangbalee,   Jai Hanuman
       Dm              F
Sankata Mochan   kripaa nidhaan
       Dm              F
Sankata Mochan   kripaa nidhaan
```

```
          C              F
Jai Jai Jai Hanuman   Gosaaee
        C                  F
Kripaa karahu Gurudeva   kee naaee
       Dm              F
Sankata Mochan   kripaa nidhaan,
       Dm              F
Laala Langotta,   Laala Nishaan
```

```
            C                              F
Hare Raama Raama Raama, Seetaa Raama Raama Raama
```

Jai Hanuman

D G A7

Jai SitaRam
Jai Hanuman

Jai SitaRam
Jai Hanuman

Jai Hanuman
Jai Hanuman

Jai Hanuman
Jai Hanuman

Ring the Bells (8x)

Ring the Bells
That still can ring
Forget your perfect offering
There is a crack, a crack in everything
That's how the light,
That's how the light gets in...

So Ring the Bells

Jai SitaRam
Jai Hanuman...

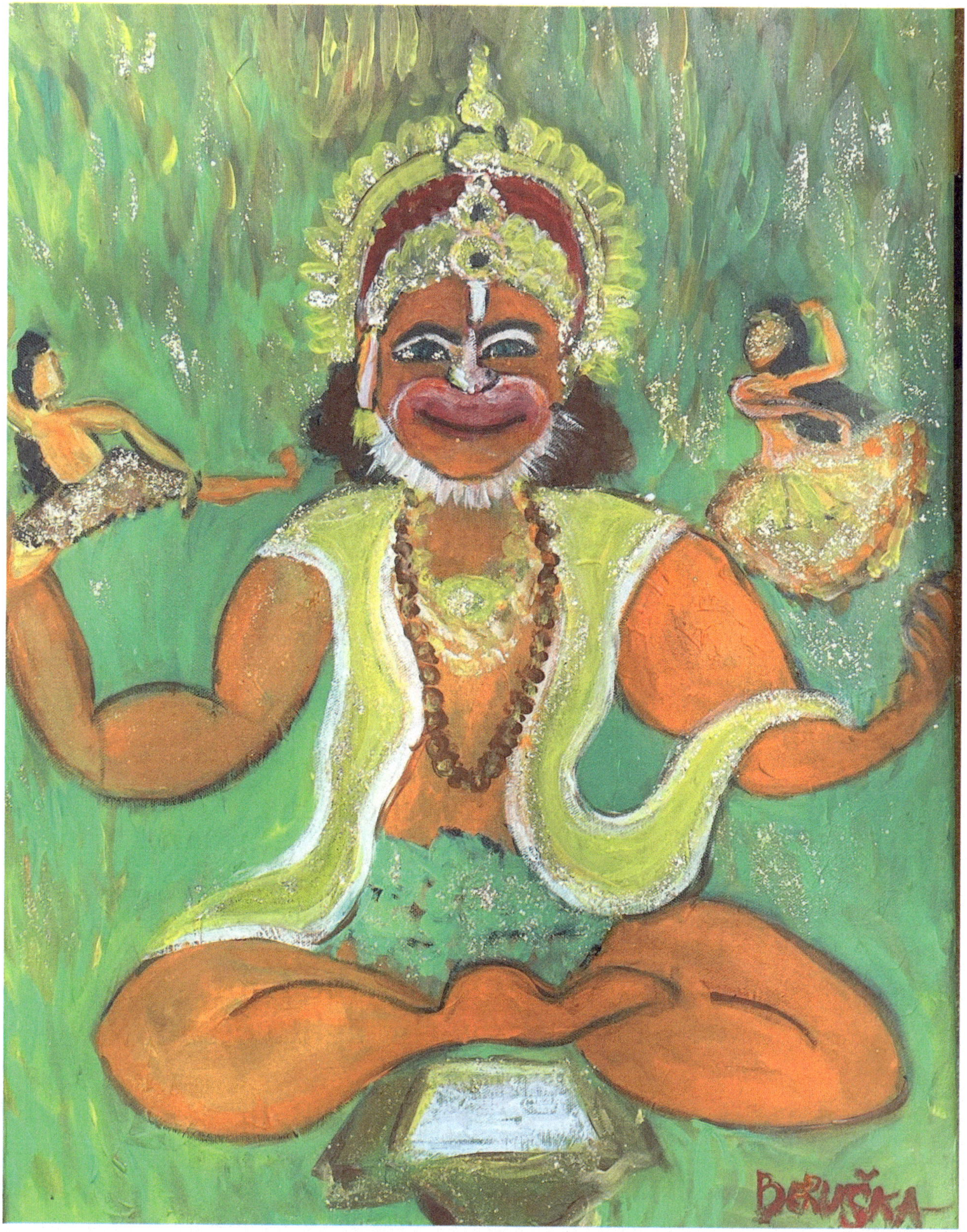
BERUŠKA

Shree Hanuman Chaleesa

(Invocation)
Shree Guru charana saroja raja
nija manu mukuru sudhari
Baranaun Raghubara bimala jasu
jo daayaku phala chaari

Having polished the mirror of my heart with the dust of my Guru's lotus feet
I sing the pure fame of the best of Raghus, which bestows the four fruits of life.

Budhi heena tanu jaanike sumiraun pawana kumaara
Bala budhi vidyaa dehu mohin harahu kalesa bikaara

I know that this body of mine has no intelligence, so I recall you, Son of the Wind
Grant me strength, wit and wisdom and remove my sorrows and shortcomings.

Bhajelo Ji Hanuman! Bhajelo Ji Hanuman!
Oh Friend! Remember Hanuman!

(Verses)
1. Jaya Hanumaan gyaana guna saagara
Jaya Kapeesha tihun loka ujaagara

Hail to Hanuman, the ocean of wisdom and virtue,
Hail Monkey Lord, illuminater of the three worlds.

2. Raama doota atulita bala dhaamaa
Anjani putra Pawanasuta naamaa

You are Ram's emissary, and the abode of matchless power
Anjani's son, named the "Son of the Wind."

3. Mahaabeera bikrama bajarangee
Kumati niwaara sumati ke sangee

Great hero, you are as mighty as a thunderbolt,
You remove evil thoughts and are the companion of the good.

**4. Kanchana barana biraaja subesaa
Kaanana kundala kunchita kesaa**

Golden hued and splendidly adorned
With heavy earrings and curly locks.

**5. Haata bajra aura dwajaa biraajai
Kaandhe moonja janeu saajai**

In your hands shine mace and a banner
And a sacred thread adorns your shoulder.

**6. Shankara suwana Kesaree nandana
Teja prataapa mahaa jaga bandana**

You are Shiva's son and Kesari's joy
And your glory is revered throughout the world.

**7. Bidyaawaana gunee ati chaatura
Raama kaaja karibe ko aatura**

You are the wisest of the wise, virtuous and clever
And ever intent on doing Ram's work.

**8. Prabhu charitra sunibe ko rasiyaa
Raama Lakhana Seetaa mana basiyaa**

You delight in hearing of the Lord's deeds,
Ram, Sita and Lakshman dwell in your heart.

**9. Sookshma roopa dhari Siyahin dikhaawaa
Bikata roopa dhari Lankaa jaraawaa**

Assuming a tiny form you appeared to Sita
And in an awesome form you burned Lanka.

**10. Bheema roopa dhari asura sanghaare
Raamachandra ke kaaja sanvaare**

Taking a dreadful form you slaughtered the demons
And completed Lord Ram's mission.

1. **Laaya sajeevana Lakhana jiyaaye
Shree Raghubeera harashi ura laaye**

2. Bringing the magic herb you revived Lakshman
And Ram embraced you with delight.

**12. Raghupati keenhee bahuta baraaee
Tuma mama priya Bharatahi sama bhaaee**

The Lord of the Raghus praised you greatly:
"Brother, you are dear to me as Bharat!"

**13. Sahasa badana tumharo jasa gaawai
Asa kahi Shreepati kanta lagaawai**

"May the thousand-mouthed serpent sing your fame!"
So saying, Lakshmi's Lord drew you to Himself.

**14. Sanakaadika Brahmaadi muneesaa
Naarada Saarada sahita Aheesaa**

Sanak and the sages, Brahma, gods and the great saints,
Narada, Saraswati and the King of serpents,

**15. Yama Kubera digapaala jahaante
Kabi kobida kahi sake kahaante**

Yama, Kubera and the guardians of the four quarters,
poets and scholars – none can express your glory.

**16. Tuma upakaara Sugreevahin keenhaa
Raama milaaya raaja pada deenhaa**

You did great service for Sugriva,
Presenting him to Ram, you gave him the kingship.

**17. Tumharo mantra Bibheeshana maanaa
Lankeshwara bhaye saba jaga jaanaa**

Vibhishana heeded your counsel
And became the Lord of Lanka, as the whole world knows.

**18. Yuga sahasra yojana para bhaanu
Leelyo taahi madhura phala jaanu**

Though the sun is thousands of miles away,
You swallowed it, thinking it to be a sweet fruit

**19. Prabhu mudrikaa meli mukha maaheen
Jaladhi laanghi gaye acharaja naaheen**

Holding the Lord's ring in your mouth
It's no surprise that you leapt over the ocean.

**20. Durgama kaaja jagata ke jete
Sugama anugraha tumhare tete**

Every difficult task in this world
Becomes easy by your grace.

**21. Raama duaare tuma rakhawaare
Hota na aagyaa binu paisaare**

You are the guardian at Ram's door,
No one enters without your leave.

**22. Saba sukha lahai tumhaaree sharanaa
Tuma rakshaka kaahu ko daranaa**

Those who take refuge in you find all happiness
and those who you protect know no fear.

**23. Aapana teja samhaaro aapai
Teenon loka haanka ten kaanpai**

You alone can withstand your own splendor,
The three worlds tremble at your roar.

**24. Bhoota pisaacha nikata nahin aawai
Mahaabeera jaba naama sunaawai**

Ghosts and goblins cannot come near,
Great Hero, when your name is uttered.

**25. Naasai roga hare saba peeraa
Japata nirantara Hanumata beeraa**

All disease and pain is eradicated,
Brave Hanuman, by constant repetition of your name.

**26. Sankata ten Hanumaana churaawai
Mana krama bachana dhyaana jo laawai**

Hanuman releases from affliction
those who remember him in thought word and deed.

**27. Saba para Raama tapaswee raajaa
Tina ke kaaja sakala tuma saajaa**

Ram, the ascetic, reigns over all,
but you carry out all his work.

**28. Aura manorata jo koee laawai
Soee amita jeewana phala paawai**

One who comes to you with any yearning
obtains the abundance of the Four Fruits of Life.

**29. Chaaron juga parataapa tumhaaraa
Hai parasidha jagata ujiyaaraa**

Your splendor fills the four ages
your glory is renowned throughout the world.

**30. Saadhu santa ke tuma rakhawaare
Asura nikandana Raama dulaare**

You are the guardian of saints and sages,
the destroyer of demons and the darling of Ram.

**31. Ashta siddhi nau nidhi ke daataa
Asa bara deena Jaanakee Maataa**

You grant the eight powers and the nine treasures
by the boon you received from Mother Janaki.

**32. Raama rasaayana toomhare paasaa
Sadaa raho Raghupati ke daasaa**

You hold the elixir of Ram's name
and remain eternally his servant.

**33. Tumhare bhajana Raama ko paawai
Janama janama ke dukha bisaraawai**

Singing your praise, one finds Ram
and escapes the sorrows of countless lives.

**34. Anta kaala Raghubara pura jaaee
Jahaan janama Hari bhakta kahaaee**

At death one goes to Ram's own city
or is born on the earth as God's devotee.

**35. Aura devataa chitta na dharaaee
Hanumata se-ee sarva sukha karaee**

Give no thought to any other deity,
worshipping Hanuman, one gains all delight.

**36. Sankata katai mite saba peeraa
Jo sumire Hanumata bala beeraa**

All affliction ceases and all pain is removed
by remembering the mighty hero, Hanuman.

**37. Jai jai jai Hanumaana Gosaaee
Kripaa karahu gurudeva kee naaee**

Victory, Victory, Victory to Lord Hanuman!
Bestow your grace on me, as my Guru!

**38. Jo sata baara paata kara koee
Chootahi bandi mahaa sukha hoee**

Whoever recites this a hundred times
is released from bondage and gains bliss.

**39. Jo yaha parai Hanumaana chaleesaa
Hoya siddhi saakhee Gaureesaa**

One who reads this Hanuman Chaleesa
gains success, as Gauri's Lord (Shiva) is witness.

**40. Tulasee Daasa sadaa Hari cheraa
Keejai naata hridaya mahan deraa**

Says Tulsi Das, who always remains Hari's servant:
"Lord, make your home in my heart."
**Pawanatanaya sankata harana mangala moorati roopa
Raama Lakhana Seetaa sahita hridaya basahu sura bhoopa**

Son of the Wind, destroyer of sorrow, embodiment of blessing,
Live in my

gururbrahma gururviṣṇu gururdevo maheśvaraḥ
guruḥ sākṣāt parabrahmā tasmai śrī gurave namaḥ

गुरुर्ब्रह्म गुरुर्विष्णु गुरुर्देवो महेश्वरः ।
गुरुः साक्षात् परब्रह्मा तस्मै श्री गुरवे नमः ॥

The Guru is Brahma, Vishnu, and Lord Shiva.
I bow to that Guru, the Supreme Being right before my eyes.

guru: teacher, spiritual preceptor, remover of darkness and ignorance
brahma: the Lord of creation
viṣnu: The Lord of preservation
maheśvara: N. of Lord Shiva, he who dissolves or destroys
sākṣāt: before one's eyes, clearly, visibly
parabrahmā: the Supreme Spirit, the Ablsolute
tasmai: unto that
śrī: lustre, splendor, radiance; respectful title
namaḥ: I bow

Love is the Strongest Medicine

OTHER MANTRAS

Buddha
Om Mani Padme Hum

Homage to the jewel in the lotus (Tibetan Buddhist)

Lakshmi
Om Shree Lakshmyai Namaha

I bow to Lakshmi, Goddess of Abundance, consort of Vishnu, who reminds me that my true nature is wholly Abundant in all ways. I need nothing.

Rama
Om Ram Ramaya Namaha

I bow to Lord Ram, who is none other than Vishnu, the preserver and maintainer of dharma

OM Shree Ram Jai Ram Jai Jai Ram!

Hanuman
Om Ham Hanumate Rudratmakaya Hoom Phat Swaha

Traditional mantra to Hanuman, the greatest devotee, incarnation of Shiva, servant of Rama & Sita, hero of the Ramayana. Hanuman reminds us that at heart we just want to see all as ourselves and finally return home, and we do that through pure devotion and dedication.

Kali
Om Kleem Kalikaye Namaha

I bow to the Dark Mother who removes our darkness, to reveal the Light that is beyond all the darkness of this world.

Krishna

Om Namo Narayanaya

Om Namo Bhagavate Vasudevaya

So Hum Hum Saha

I Am That, That I Am. I Am You, You Are Me.

Lokah Samasta

Om Lokah Samastah Sukhinoh Bhavantu

May everyone, everywhere be happy & free!

Chakra Mantras

Lam (Muladhara) ~ Vam (Swadhisthana) ~ Ram (Manipura) ~ Yam (Anahata) ~ Ham (Vishuddha) ~ Aum (Ajna) ~ Silence (Sahasrara)

Purification Mantra

Om apavitraha pavitrowah/

sarwavashtan gatopi wah/

ya smaret pundarikaksham/

sa bahya bhyantraha soocheehee

This mantra comes from my teacher Dharma Mittra and is for purifying oneself and one's environment before beginning a practice or undertaking.

Aham Prema

I Am Love

Jai Ma

Victory to the Devine Mother!

Hari Om Tat Sat

And God, ain't that the truth!

Bhajamana Ma

C G G

Bhajamana Ma Ma Ma Ma (4x)

Anandamayi Ma Ma
Anandarupa Ma Ma (2x)

O My Mind,
Sing "MA MA MA"

Bhajamana = Sing O My Mind!
Ma = Divine Mother
Ananda = Bliss
Mayi = Full
Rupa = Form
Jai = Victory!

Sing, O my mind! Sing to Mother Devine!
Mother is the Embodiment of Bliss
Yea, She verily is the very Form of Bliss itself!
She's a Mother like no Other!

*"You can't change the world,
you can only change your mind..."*

*"You can't change it, girl,
you can only learn to be more kind..."*

OM Namo Narayanaya

OM Namo Narayanaya
OM Namo Narayanaya

Sonny said when he was just 2 years old
"There's nothing happenin' at all."
Whenever he turned on that Daddy-O
There was nothin' goin' down at all
Then one morning he turned on
that Mommy station
he couldn't believe what he heard at all
he started dancing to that fine fine music
you know his life was saved by Rock n Roll.
Despite all the Amputations
You could dance to a Rock n Roll station
& it was alright
It was alri

Chamundayai Kali Ma

Chamundayai Kali Ma
Kali Ma
Kali Ma
Kali Ma (4x)

Aum Ayeem Hreem Kleem
Chamundayai Veechey (4x)

Kali Ma
Kali Ma
Kali Ma
Kali Ma

Aum Ayeem Hreem Kleem
Chamundayai Veechey (4x)

Are we really happy here?

Durge Jai Jai Ma

Am G F Am

Durge Durge Durge Jai Jai Ma

Ananda Sagari Ma

Karuna Sagari Ma

Kali Kapalini Ma

Jagadodharini Ma

Jaya Durge Jai Jai Ma!

The answer is within you!

Twameva

Tvam-Eva Maataa Ca Pitaa Tvam-Eva

|Tvam-Eva Bandhush-Ca Sakhaa Tvam-Eva |

Tvam-Eva Viidyaa Dravinnam Tvam-Eva |

Tvam-Eva Sarvam Mama Deva Deva ||

You are my Mother And You are my Father.

You are my Lover And my Beloved Friend.

You are True Knowledge & You are True Wealth.

You are Everything

My All in All!

tvameva mātā ca pitā tvameva
tvameva bandhuśca sakhā tvameva
tvameva vidyā draviṇam tvameva
tvameva sarvam mama deva deva

त्वमेव माता च पिता त्वमेव ।
त्वमेव बन्धुश्च सखा त्वमेव ।
त्वमेव विद्या द्रविणम् त्वमेव ।
त्वमेव सर्वम् मम देव देव ॥

You are my mother and my father.
You are my family and my friend.
You are my knowledge and my wealth.
You are my All, God of Gods!

tvam: you
eva: certainly
mātṛ: mother
ca: and
pitṛ: father
bandhu: relative, kinsman, family
sakha: friend
vidyā: knowledge, learning
draviṇa: wealth, money, propery
sarva: all, every, entire, whole
mama: my
deva: god

60

kāyena vācā manasendriyairvā
buddhyātmanā vā prakṛteḥ svabhāvāt
karomi yadyatsakalaṁ parasmai
guruvarāyeti samarpayāmi

कायेन वाचा मनसेन्द्रियैर्वा
बुद्ध्यात्मना वा प्रकृतेः स्वभावात् ।
करोमि यद्यत्सकलं परस्मै
गुरुवरायेति समर्पयामि ॥

Whatever actions I may perform,
by body, mind, senses, intellect,
soul, character, or by the force of Nature,
I offer all to the greatest of teachers.

kāyena: by the body
vācā: speech
manas: mind, intellect, intelligence
indriya: senses
vā: or
buddhi: mind, thought
ātman: the soul
prakṛti: original source, primary substance, Nature
svabhāva: one's natural disposition
karomi: I do or make
yadyat: whatever
sakalaṁ: everything
parasmai: to the best, greatest, highest
guru: teacher, spiritual preceptor, remover of darkness or ignorance
iti: places emphasis on what precedes
samarpayāmi: I offer, bestow, present

Sarva Mangala

Sarva Mangala Mangalye
Shive Sarvatha Sadikei
Sharanyei Tryambakei Gauri
Narayani Namostute x2
(Om Namah Shivaya. . . .)

Oh Great Feminine power of Shiva, Narayani,
whose very touch brings ecstasy,
one who opens the eye of wisdom,
bestow upon us the highest blessings."

om sarveśāṁ svastirbhavatu
sarveśāṁ śāntirbhavatu
sarveśāṁ pūrṇam bhavatu
sarveśāṁ maṅgalaṁ bhavatu

ॐ सर्वेषां स्वस्तिर्भवतु ।
सर्वेषां शान्तिर्भवतु ।
सर्वेषां पूर्णं भवतु ।
सर्वेषां मङ्गलं भवतु ॥

Auspiciousness be unto all.
Perfect peace be unto all.
Fullness be unto all.
Prosperity be unto all.

om: sacred syllable often at the commencement of prayers
sarva: all, entire, every
svasti: well-being, success, fortune
bhavatu: may there be
śānti: peace, tranquility
pūrṇa: full, content, satisfied
maṅgala: happiness, felicity, welfare

Om Namah Shivaya
(Robert Gass)

G C Am G

Om Namah Shivaya

Om Namah Shivaya

Om Namah Shivaya

Shiva Om Namah

I bow to Śiva, the Auspicious One,
the Great God who is the Lord of Yoga,
and is another name for the guru,
the master teacher, who resides within me.

Called the Great God (Mahadeva), the Lord of Yoga, the Cosmic Dancer (Nataraja), the Destroyer, among thousands of other names, Shiva primarily embodies stillness in dynamism, and is the energy of dissolving the ego/universe to bring it back to its original oneness.

Show Me the Way

(Camille Archer)

A -> D

Guru Guru Show Me the Way

Doesn't Matter If You Follow the Rules

As Long as you follow the truth

I feel you in my heart

I feel you in my soul

OM Namo Bhagavate Vasudevaya (2x)

SitaRama SitaRam

SitaRama Sitaram

Shiva Shambho

Am G F
Shiva Shiva Shiva
Shiva Shambho
Shiva Shiva Shiva
Shiva Shambho

Om Namah Shivaya
Om Namah Shivaya
Om Namah Shivaya
Om Namah Shivaya (2x)

With an everlasting cry
We die before we die
Into the sacred fire
Singing Om Namah Shivaya

Om Namah Shivaya
Om Namah Shivaya
Om Namah Shivaya
Om Namah Shivaya

Original Dread

A C#m7 G Bm7
Om Namah Shivaya
Om Namah Shivaya
Om Namah Shivaya
Shivaya Namah Om (3x)

Jaya Jaya Shiva Shambho
Jaya Jaya Shiva Shambho
Mahadeva Shambho
Mahadeva Shambho

Om Namah Shivaya
Om Namah Shivaya
Om Namah Shivaya
Shivaya Namah Om (3x)

Hara Hara Shiva Shambho
Hara Hara Shiva Shambho
Mahadeva Shambho
Mahadeva Shambho

This goes out to the Original Dread!
The goes out to the Origina DreadHead
Shiva Maharaj
True Rasta
Yoga Masta
So let's all lift our voice to the Sun
To the One, to the place in heart where it's
Already undone

Shiva Bolo-ro

Hai Shiva Shankara (Alan)
Call / Response
F# / G
Hai Shiva Shankara 2x
F# / G
Hara Shiva Om Kara 2x
G
Jai Shiva Shambo Shankara
F#
Nama Shivaya 2x

F#   G   F#
Hara Om Nama Shivaya 2x
G
Nama Shivaya Nama Shivaya
F#
Nama Shivaya Om 2x

Bm   A
Hai Shiva Shambo Shankara
G   A
Nama Shivaya 2x

Bolo Bolo Sabamila Bolo

Bm A G

Bolo bolo sabamila bolo
Om Namah Shivaya

Bolo bolo sabamila bolo
Om Namah Shivaya

Om Namah Shivaya
Om Namah Shivaya

Mrtyunjaya Mantra

Em. Fmaj7 F#maj7
Om trayambakam yajamahe
sugandhim pushti vardhanam
urvaarukamiva bandhanan
mrtyor mookshiya mamrtat

I pray to the three-eyed one (Shiva),
who is none other than my inner guru,
to help me realize the Self
& thus attain liberation
From attachment & suffering

Mahāmṛtyuñjaya Mantra
om tryambakaṁ yajāmahe sugandhiṁ puṣṭivardhanam
urvārukamiva bandhanānmṛtyormukṣīya mā'mṛtāt

महामृत्युञ्जय मन्त्र
ॐ त्र्यम्बकं यजामहे सुगन्धिं पुष्टिवर्धनम् ।
उर्वारुकमिव बन्धनान्मृत्योर्मुक्षीय माऽमृतात् ॥

Great Victory over Death Mantra
We worship the All-Seeing One.
Fragrant, He nourishes bounteously.
May I be free from the fear of death
like the fruit of the vine freed from its stem,
but not from the nectar of immortality.

mahā: great, powerful
mṛtyu: death
jaya: victory, conquest
mantra: "instrument of thought", sacred speech
om: sacred syllable often at the commencement of prayers
tri: three
ambaka: eye
yajāmahe: we worship
sugandhi: sweet-smelling, fragrant
puṣṭivardhana: increasing, growing
urvāruka: cucumber, fruit of a vine
iva: like, in the same manner as
bandhanāt: from the stem
mṛtyu: death
mukṣīya: may I be free or released from
mā: not
amṛtāt: from immortality

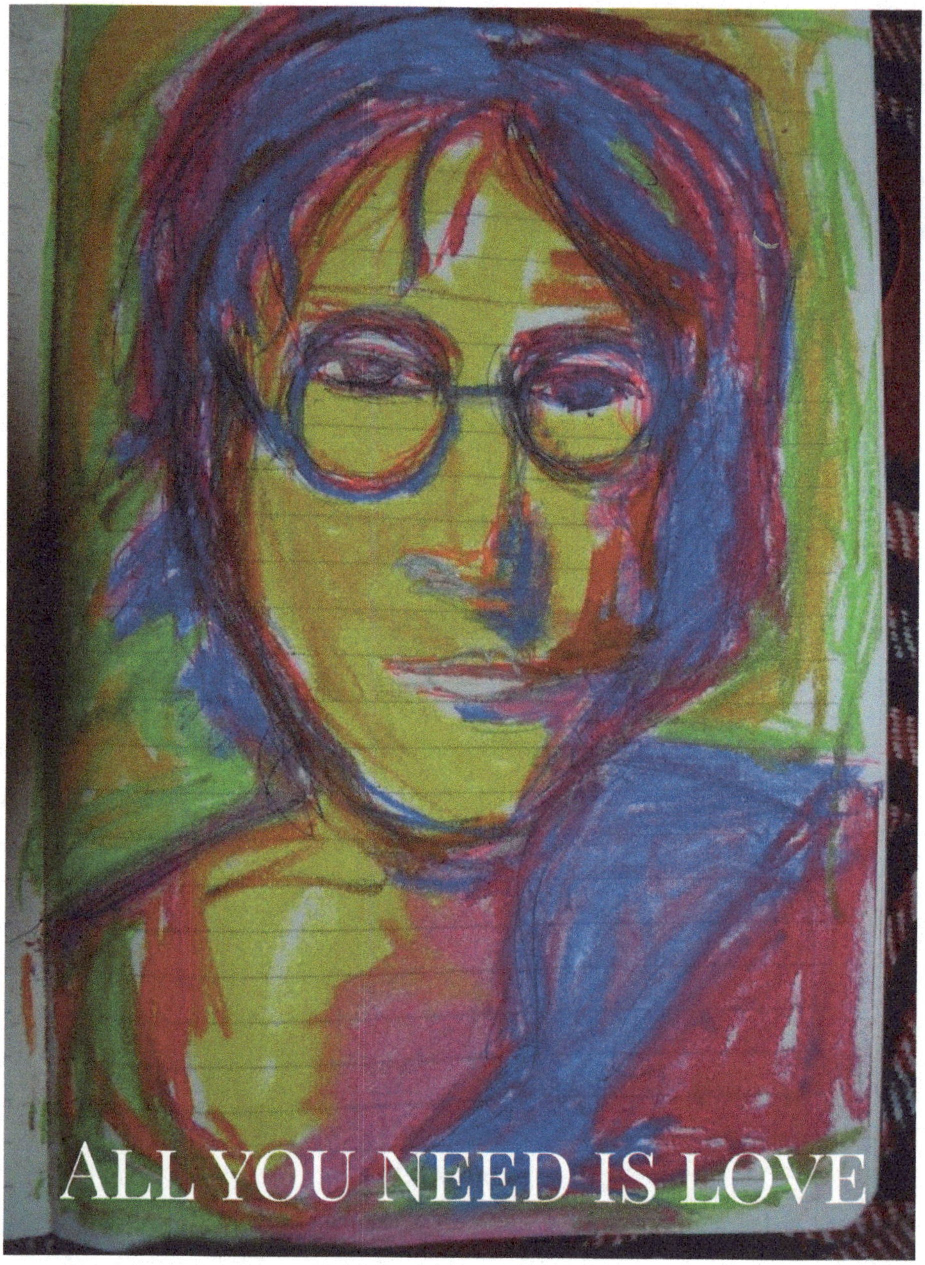
ALL YOU NEED IS LOVE

karpūragauraṁ karuṇāvatāraṁ
saṁsārasāram bhujagendrahāram
sadāvasantaṁ hṛdayāravinde
bhavaṁ bhavānīsahitaṁ namāmi

कर्पूरगौरं करुणावतारं
संसारसारम् भुजगेन्द्रहारम् ।
सदावसन्तं हृदयारविन्दे
भवं भवानीसहितं नमामि ॥

Pure white like camphor, the incarnation of compassion,
the essence of existence, whose necklace is the king of serpents,
always dwelling in the lotus of the heart,
to Siva and Shakti, I bow.

karpūra: camphor
gaura: white, shining, brilliant
karuṇa: compassion
āvatāra: appearance or incarnation of any deity upon earth
saṁsāra: course or passage (of the embodied soul), the world
sāra: the source or essence
bhujaga: snake, serpent
indra: the best, excellent, chief
hāra: garland, necklace
sadā: always, perpetually
vas: to dwell or stay
hṛdaya: the heart, the most dear or secret part of anything
aravinda: lotus
bhavaṁ: pure being, existence, Siva
bhavānī: N. of Parvati (wife of Siva), Sakti
sahita: together
namāmi: I bow

Tat Tvam Asi ~ That Thou Art

D A7 -> G D A D

From Joy we came
In joy we live
To joy we shall return

Tat Tvam Asi
Tat Tvam Asi

& That Thou Art
That Thou Art
That Thou Art
That Thou Art

The Joy of the heart
The joy in your heart!

Jai Jai Ma
Jai Jai Ma
Jai Jai Ma

तत्त्वमसि ।
tat tvam asi

Raghupati Raghav Rajaram

Raghupati Raghav Rajaram
Patit Paavan Sitaram

Sitaram Jai Sitaram
Bhaj pyare tu Sitaram
Raghupati.........

Ishwar Allah Tere Naam
Sabko sanmati de Bhagwan
Raghupati ....

Raat ko Nindiya Din ko Kaam
Kabhi Bhajoge Prabhu Ka Naam
Karte rahiye aapne Kaam
Lete Rahiye Prabhu Ka Naam

Raghupati Raghav
Rajaram Patit Paavan Sitaram

रघुपति राघव राजा राम

पतित पावन सीता राम

सीता राम सीता राम

भज प्यारे तू सीता राम

रघुपति ...

ईश्वर अल्लाह तेरे नाम
सबको सन्मति दे भगवान
रघुपत

रात को निंदिया दिन तो काम
कभी भजोगे प्रभु का नाम
करते रहिये अपने काम
लेते रहिये हरि का नाम
रघुपति ...

Ishvar Allah Tero naam means – People call you by many names,
some call you God "Ishvar" while some call you Allah,
but you are the one and only the Brahman,
infinite Divinity that is within us all and we are all within you.

Om Poornamadaha
(from the Isha Upanishad)

G C D

Om Poornamada(ha) Poornamidam

Poornat Poorna Mudachyate

Poornasya Poornam'aadayaa

Poornameva Vashishyate

Om Namo Narayanaya

That is Perfect, This is Perfect

From Perfection, Perfection Comes

Take Perfection from Perfection

& Only Perfection Remains

MEDICINE SONGS

Ayawaska Takimuyki

[Verso 1]
Ayawaska urkumanta
Takiy, takiymuyki
Ayawaska urkumanta
Takiy, takiymuyki

Ch'uya, ch'uya hampuykuyni
Misk'i, ñucñu cuerpo chayta
Ch'uya, ch'uya hampuykuyni
Misk'i, ñucñu cuerpo chayta
Ch'uya, ch'uya hampuykuyni
Misk'i, ñucñu cuerpo chayta

[Verso 2]
Ayawaska curandera
Takiy, takiymuyki
Ayawaska curandera
Takiy, takiymuyki

Ch'uya, ch'uya hampuykuyni
Misk'i, ñucñu cuerpo chayta
Ch'uya, ch'uya hampuykuyni
Misk'i, ñucñu cuerpo chayta
Ch'uya, ch'uya hampuykuyni
Misk'i, ñucñu cuerpo chayta

[Verso 3]
Ayawaska luceritomanta
Takiy, takiymuyki
Ayawaska luceritomanta
Takiy, takiymuyki

Ch'uya, ch'uya hampuykuyni
Misk'i, ñucñu cuerpo chayta
Ch'uya, ch'uya hampuykuyni
Misk'i, ñucñu cuerpo chayta
Ch'uya, ch'uya hampuykuyni
Misk'i, ñucñu cuerpo chayta

[Verso 4]
Ayawaska chacrunera
Takiy, takiymuyki
Ayawaska chacrunera
Takiy, takiymuyki

Ch'uya, ch'uya hampuykuyni
Misk'i, ñucñu cuerpo chayta
Ch'uya, ch'uya hampuykuyni
Misk'i, ñucñu cuerpo chayta
Ch'uya, ch'uya hampuykuyni
Misk'i, ñucñu cuerpo chayta

[Verso 5]
Ayawaska pinturera
Takiy, takiymuyki
Ayawaska pinturera
Takiy, takiymuyki

Ch'uya, ch'uya hampuykuyni
Misk'i, ñucñu cuerpo chayta
Ch'uya, ch'uya hampuykuyni
Misk'i, ñucñu cuerpo chayta
Ch'uya, ch'uya hampuykuyni
Misk'i, ñucñu cuerpo chayta

[Verso 6]
Ayawaska curandera
Takiy, takiymuyki
Ayawaska curandera
Takiy, takiymuyki

Ch'uya, ch'uya hampuykuyni
Misk'i, ñucñu cuerpo chayta
Ch'uya, ch'uya hampuykuyni
Misk'i, ñucñu cuerpo chayta
Ch'uya, ch'uya hampuykuyni
Misk'i, ñucñu cuerpo chayta

Hermoso Espiritu

Hermoso espíritu del agua llega ya
curando, purificando llega ya

hermoso pájaro del agua llega ya
curando, purificando llega ya

hermoso espíritu del cielo llega ya
curando, iluminando llega ya

hermoso espiritu ayahuasca llega ya

hermoso espiritu pachamama llega ya

hermoso espiritu kambocito llega ya

En el corazón de este fuego soplan ya
cuatro vientos en el centro soplan ya
en el corazón de este fuego brillan ya
siete flechas en el centro brillan ya

En el corazón de este fuego vuelan ya
la gran águila del cielo vuela ya
el gran cóndor de los Andes vuela ya

Aqua De Estrellas

D F C G
En tus ojos de agua infinita
Se bañan las estrellitas, mamá
En tus ojos de agua infinita
Se bañan las estrellitas, mamá

Agua de luz, agua de estrellas
Pachamama, viene del cielo
Agua de luz, agua de estrellas
Pachamama, viene del cielo

Limpia, limpia, limpia corazón
Agua brillante
Sana, sana, sana corazón
Agua bendita
Calma, calma, calma corazón
Agua del cielo
Mamá

En tus ojos de agua infinita
Se bañan las estrellitas, mamá
En tus ojos de agua infinita
Se bañan las estrellitas, mamá

Agua de luz, agua de estrellas
Pachamama, viene del cielo
Agua de luz, agua de estrellas
Pachamama, viene del cielo

Limpia, limpia, limpia corazón
Agua brillante
Sana, sana, sana corazón
Agua bendita
Calma, calma, calma corazón
Agua del cielo
Mamá

Tribus

Ayahuasca Tribu curacaini - Ayahuasca tribe of healers
Shamuri - come, come, come
Ayahuasca Tribu curacaini - Ayahuasca tribe of healers
Shamuri - come, come, come
Dai da dai da daa, danda da da, dai da dai da daa, danda da da
Dai da dai da daa, danda da da
Dai da da da da, dai da da daa da
Ayahuasca
Pachamama Tribu curacaini
- Pachamama tribe of healers
Shamuri - come, come, come
Pachamama Tribu curacaini - Pachamama tribe of
Healers
Shamuri - come, come, come
Dai da da da da, dai da da daa da (x2)
Tribu tribunanta medicina runa - tribes from all over the world, spirits of the medicine
Tribu tribunanta medicina runa - tribes from all over the world, spirits of the medicine
Dai da da da da, dai da da daa da (x2)
Tribu tribunanta medicina runa - tribes from all over the world, spirits of the medicine
Tribu tribunanta medicina runa - tribes from all over the world, spirits of the medicine
Medicina runa, Medicina runa
- spirit of the medicine
Impro part
Shipibo Tribu curacaini - Shipibo tribe of healers
Belgica Tribu curacaini - Belgium tribe of healers
Bora Bora Tribu curacaini
- Bora Bora tribe of healers
Yawanawa Tribu curacaini
- Yawanawa tribe of healers
Tribu Tribunanta medicina runa - tribes from all over the world, spirits of the medicine
Tribu Tribunanta medicina runa - tribes from all over the world, spirits of the medicine

Sirenita Bobinsana

C G B7 Em, G B7 Em, C G B7 Em , G B7Em ....

Sirenita del los rios danza danza con el viento (2x)

Con tus flores y aromas perfuma los corazones (2x)

Cura cura cuerpecito limpia limpia spirititu (2x)

Cantaremos icaritos, abuelita curandera

Danzaremos muy juntitos, sirenita bobinsana

dei dei da dei da dei da (2x)

nai nai na nai na nei na (2x)

Translation

Little mermaid of the river, dance, dance with the wind
WIth your flowers and aromas, perfuming our hearts
Heal, heal our little bodies, cleanse, cleanse our spirits
We will sing icaros, grandmother, healer
We will dance very close, little mermaid,

Noku Mana

Dm F Am

[Verso 1]
Noku mana e bubu bubutã
Eskawatã kaya waikiki
Noku mana e bubu bubutã
Eskawatã kaya waikiki

Eskawatã kaya
Kaya wai
Kaya wai
Kaya waikiki

Eskawatã kaya
Kaya wai
Kaya wai
Kaya waikiki

[Verso 2]
Noku niwe e bubu bubutã
Eskawatã kaya waikiki
Noku niwe e bubu bubutã
Eskawatã kaya waikiki

Eskawatã kaya
Kaya wai
Kaya wai
Kaya Waikiki

Eskawatã kaya
Kaya wai
Kaya wai
Kaya waikiki

[Break]

[Verso 3]
Noku ni e bubu bubutã
Eskawatã kaya waikiki
Noku ni e bubu bubutã
Eskawatã kaya waikiki

Eskawatã kaya
Kaya wai
Kaya wai
Kaya waikiki

Eskawatã kaya
Kaya wai
Kaya wai
Kaya waikiki

[Verso 4]
Noku bixi e bubu bubutã
Eskawatã kaya waikiki
Noku bixi e bubu bubutã

Eskawatã kaya
Kaya wai
Kaya wai
Kaya waikiki

Eskawatã kaya
Kaya wai
Kaya wai
Kaya waikiki

[Verso 5]
Noku bari e bubu bubutã
Eskawatã kaya waikiki
Noku bari e bubu bubutã
Eskawatã kaya waikiki

Eskawatã kaya
Kaya wai
Kaya wai
Kaya waikiki

Eskawatã kaya
Kaya wai
Kaya wai
Kaya waikiki

[Ponte]
Noku
Xinã e bubu
Xinã e bubu bubutã

Eskawatã kaya wai
Kaya waikiki
Kaya, kaya waikiki

Noku
Ranu e bubu
Ranu e bubu bubutã

Eskawatã kaya wai
Kaya waikiki
Kaya, kaya waikiki

Noku
Ushu e bubu
Ushu e bubu bubutã

Eskawatã kaya wai
Kaya waikiki
Kaya, kaya waikiki

Noku
Kênê e bubu
Kênê e bubu bubutã

Eskawatã kaya wai
Kaya waikiki
Kaya, kaya waikiki

Ux, ux
Aux, aux, aux, aux, aux, aux

[Verso 6]
Noku bari e bubu bubutã
Eskawatã kaya waikiki
Noku bari e bubu bubutã
Eskawatã kaya waikiki

Eskawatã kaya
Kaya wai
Kaya wai
Kaya waikiki

Eskawatã kaya
Kaya wai
Kaya wai
Kaya waikiki

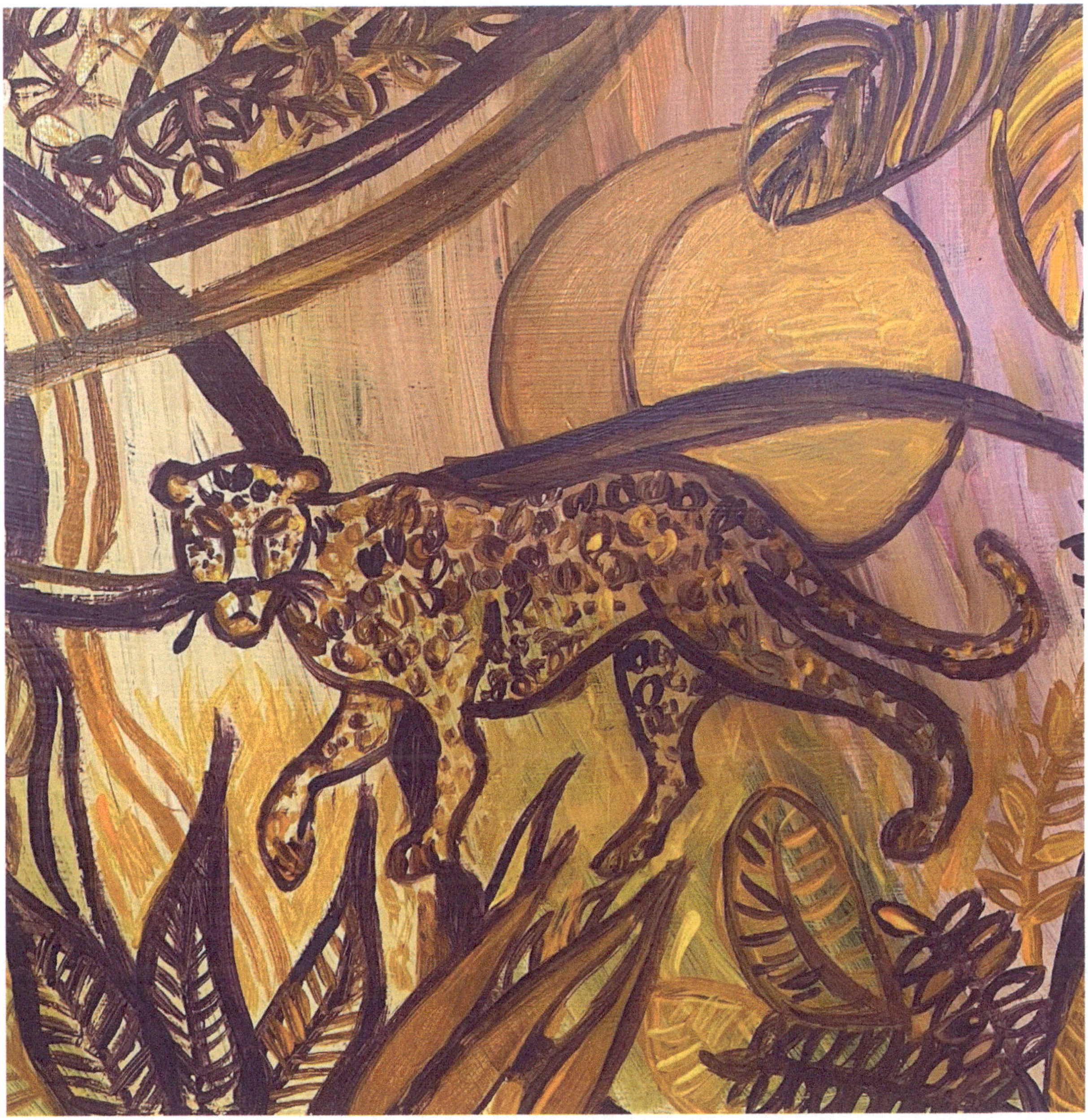

Because I Love You So Much

Hey Yana Hey Hey Yo

Hey Yana Hey Hey Yana Hey Yana Hey Yana Hey Yo

Hey Yana Hey Hey Yana Hey Yo

Hey Yana Hey Hey Yana Hey Hey Yo Hey

Shukletkutle Wawatey Yo (4x)

Hey Yana Hey Hey Yo Hey

Porque te quiero/amo tanto

Con todo mi Corazon

Hey Yana Hey Hey Yo Hey (2 x)

Because I love you so much

Because I love you so much so much so much

Because I love you so much

With all of my heart

Hey Yana Hey Hey Yo Hey

Cuñaq

Desde Cuñaq viene,
agüita serpenteando ,
por las acequias y en remolinos,
Am hacia nuestras vidas. (bis)

De cantar hualinas y a la vez llorando
toditas mis penas se acabaron
Pachamama está de fiesta. (bis)
Una estrellita que alegre me decía,

canta cantorcito a la agüita,
a la agüita madre Cuñaq.
(bis) De cantar hualinas...

Desde Kunyaq vienes, agüita serpenteando Por las acequias y en remolinos, hacia nuestras vidas

De cantar gualinas, a la vez llorando Toditas mis penas se acabaron, Pachamama esta de fiesta Una estrellita, que alegre me decía, canta cantorcito al agüita Al agüita Madre Kunyaq

Translation From Kunyaq (a sacred spring in Peru) you come, winding around Through the canals and whirlpools, into our lives Singing songs of water, and at the same time crying All my sorrows are gone, Pachamama is celebrating A little star, so happy she said, sing, little singer to the water To the water of Mother Kunyaq

Thank You for This Day
(Native American Hymn)

Thank you for this day Spirit,

Thank you for this day. (2x)

This healing, this healing, This healing day. (2x)

Thank you for this day Spirit,

Thank you for this day. (2x)

This beautiful, this beautiful, This beautiful day.

(2x)

Thank you for my friends Spirit,

Thank you for my friends. (2x)

My wonderful, my wonderful, My wonderful

friends. (2x)

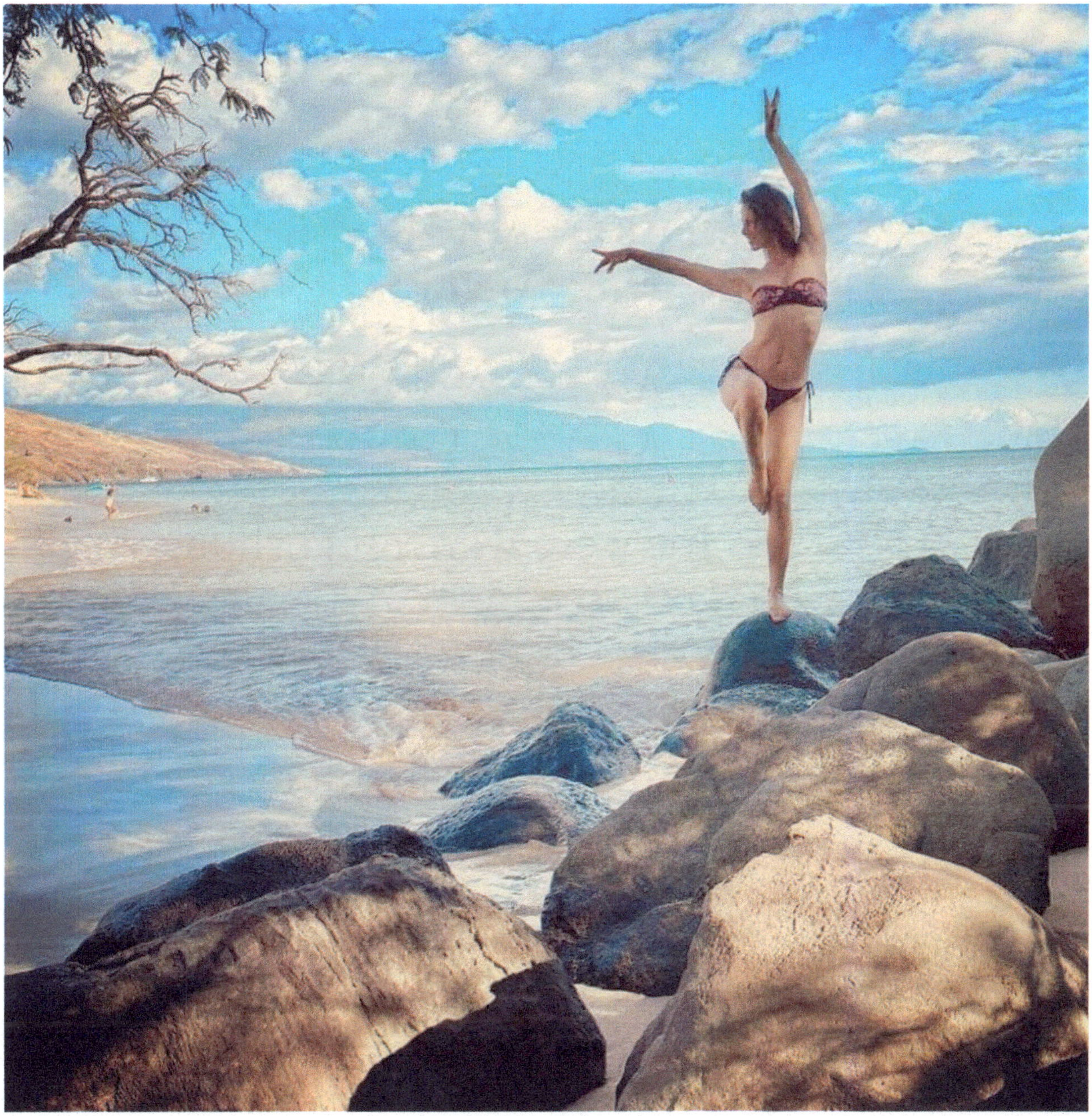

Ide Were Were

Em* Am7 Em* B7
Em* Am7 Em* C+9
Am7 —— D ——
Am7 —— B7 ——
G —— C+9 ——

Ide were were nita oshun

Ide were were

Ide were were nita oshun

Ide were were nita ya

Ocha kiniba nita oshun

Cheke cheke cheke

Nita ya

Ide were were

I Release Control
(Alexis Sunshine Rose)

I release control

And surrender to the flow

of Love that will heal me

(always healing)

Gathering the Flowers
(Devananda Lali)

Gathering the flowers
Flowers from the forest
Forest full of medicine
to help us with our healing
Healing of our bodies
Body, mind, and spirit
Spirit of the Water
come wash over my heart
My heart is growing open
Opening each moment
Each moment is a miracle
that's calling us to gather
Gathering the flowers
Flowers from the forest
Forest full of medicine
to help us with our healing
Healing of our bodies
Body, mind, and spirit
Spirit of the Water,
come wash away my tears.
Tears of joy I'm crying,
Crying for my people,
People we are ready,
Remember we are free.
Free to be new people
Beautiful empowered
Empowering each other
In peace we come to Gather...
in peace we come to Gather...

Ho'oponopono

Aloha Ke Akua

Aloha Nui Loa

Aloha Mama Aina

Aloha Sweet Ohana

*

I'm sorry

Please forgive me

Thank you

& I love you

*

Mahalo Ke Akua

Mahalo Nui Loa

Mahalo Mama Aina

Mahalo Sweet Ohana

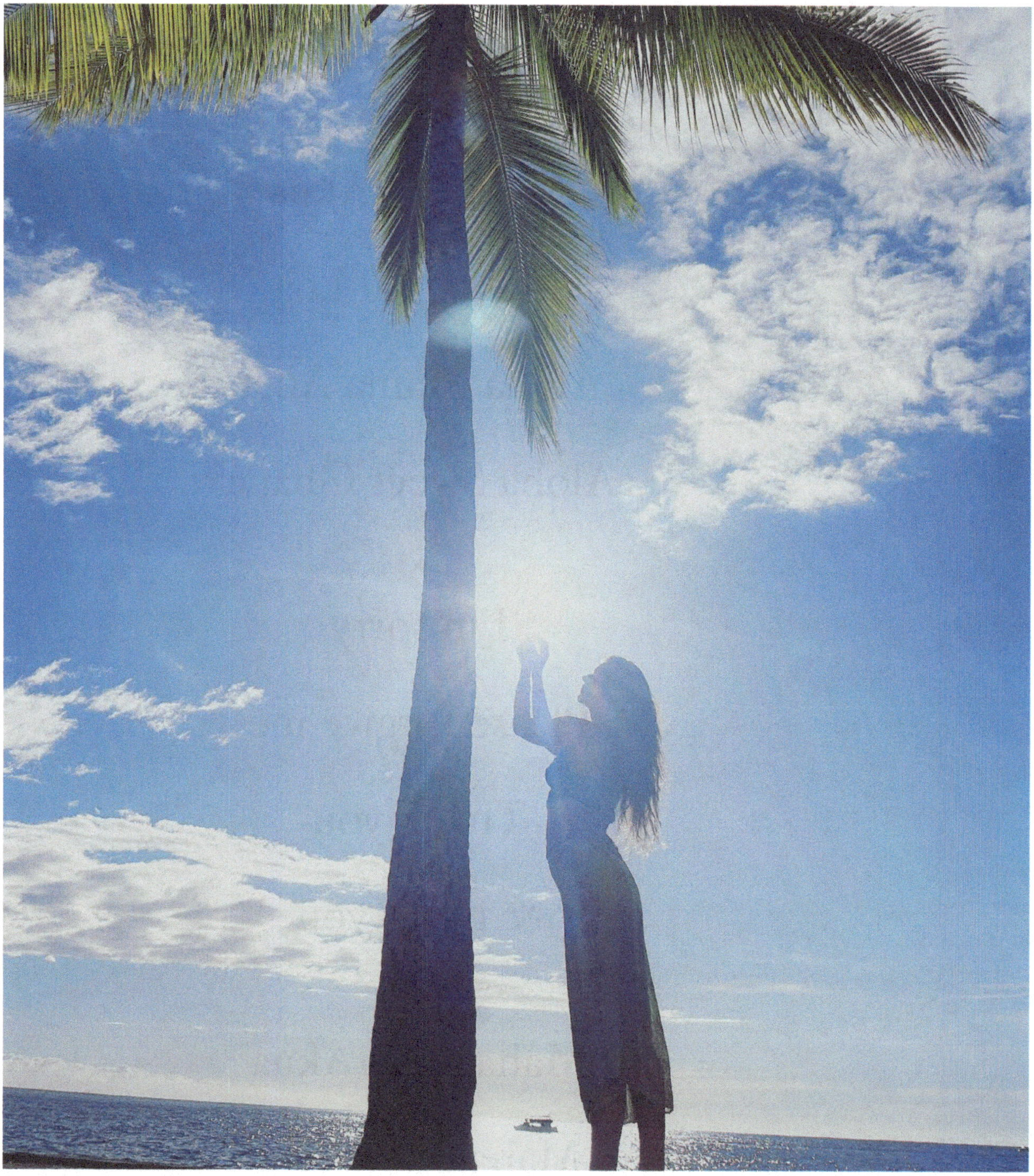

We Have Drunk Soma

These *shlokas* (verses) from the ancient Vedas regarding the sacred plant Soma are as valid now as they were when they were written.

ápāma sómam amŕtā abhūma
áganma jyótir ávidāma devā́n
kím nūnám asmā́n kr̥ṇavad árātiḥ
kím u dhūrtír amr̥ta mártiyasya[7]

We have drunk Soma
& have become immortal.
We have entered into the light,
we have found the gods!
What can hostility do to us now,
& what the malice of a mortal,
Oh immortal one.

— *Atharvashiras Upanishad, Chapter 3*[20][21]

Shaman's Drum

Rosie Emery

    Cm –   Fm -
Smokey mountain dreamer, I'm glad you came my way
There's so much I have learned from you,
    G   Cm
There's so much more to say;
You're flying with the raven, You hold the burning flame
No love is lost that can't be found, And brought to life again...
        G
You get up with the morning sun
     Cm
And listen to the rhythm of the medicine drum
     G
And you go down with the evening stars to
   Cm   Fm
Light your mind, when you live in eternity
    Cm
You have to dream your reality
    G
And as you pick up the threads, you play
   Cm
On your shaman's drum

Smokey mountain dreamer, don't let sadness cloud your eyes,
The memories that come to you, have never been disguised
For love is like the shadow, we cannot always see,
But when the light it shines through you, I feel it shine through me

Smokey mountain dreamer, don't let sadness cloud your eyes,
The memories that come to you, have never been disguised,
For love's the thread that binds us, it weaves us in its song
The breath of life that lives us, it's the beat that keeps us strong

Viva La Medicina

Am F C E7

Viva la vida sagrada
Viva la familia
Viva la musica

Viva Viva Viva
La Medicina!

Let thy medication
Be your silent meditation
The cure for every illness –
Just a little bit of stillness

Viva Viva Viva
Viva la medicina!

Viva Viva Viva
Viva la medicina!

RAINBOW FAMILY SONGS

We Are Gathering

We are gathering

Gathering together

We are singing

Singing our heartsong

This is family

This is unity

This is celebration

This is sacred

We are Opening up in Sweet Surrender

We are opening up in sweet surrender
To the luminous love light of the One. (2x)

We are opening. We are opening.
We are opening. We are opening.

We are rising up like a phoenix from the fire;
Brothers and sisters spread your wings and fly higher! (2x)

We are rising up. We are rising up.
We are rising up. We are rising up.

We are opening up like a lotus flower;
Let the love light shine in our hearts tonight. (2x)

We are opening. We are opening.
We are opening. We are opening.

We are rising up like the beat of the drum.
Beat by beat, we beat as one. (2x)

We are rising up. We are rising up.
We are rising up. We are rising up.

"Let it be known there is a fountain that was not made by the hands of men."

We Are One in Harmony

D C G

We are one in harmony
Singing in celebration

We are one in harmony
Singing in love

We are one in harmony
Singing in celebration

We are one in harmony
Singing in love

We are one
Singing in celebration

We are one
Singing in love

The River is Flowing

Em -> D
The river is flowing, flowing and growing
The river is flowing back to the sea
Mother, carry me, your child I will always be
Mother, carry me back to the sea

(other verses...)

The moon she is waning, waxing and waning
The moon she is waiting for us to be free
Sister moon watch over me your child I will always be
Sister moon watch over me until we are free

The sun he is shining, rising and shining
The sun he is shining to brighten our way
Father sun shine over me your child I will always be
Father sun shine over me and brighten our way

The fire is burning, destroying and burning
The fire is burning for us to get pure
Violet flame burn over me a child I will always be
Violet flame burn over me until I am pure

Universal Lover
(Fantuzzi)

You're my mother
You're my father
You're my lover
You are my friend
You are the beginning
You are the center
And you are beyond the end

You are the colors of the rainbow
You're the pure white light in me
You are the rivers and the mountains
Lord, you are the sky, you are the sea

And I love you so
You help me see
See you in all
Is to see you in me

I'm in you and you're in me
I'm in you and you're in me
I'm in you and you're in me
I'm in you and you're in me

Petals of a lotus
Are many
But the lotus is one

Branches of a tree
There are many
But the tree is one

Teachers and teachings
Are many
But the Truth is one

Prophets and religions
They are many
But God is one

And I love you so
You help me see
See you in all
Is to see you in me

I'm in you and you're in me
I'm in you and you're in me
I'm in you and you're in me
I'm in you and you're in me

I want to touch you
I want to feel you
Lord I want to be right by your side

I want to know you

Love you
I want to serve you all the time

'Cause you're my mother
You are my father
You are my lover
You are my friend
You are the beginning
You are the center
And you are beyond the end

I love you so
You help me see (Lord, you helped me see)
See you in all
Is to see you in me (See you in me)

I'm in you and you're in me (Holy Mother)
I'm in you and you're in me
I'm in you and you're in me (Holy Father)
I'm in you and you're in me

I'm in you and you're in me
(You make me so happy)
I'm in you and you're in me
Divine energy
I'm in you and you're in me
Oh yeah

I'm in you and you're in me
I'm in you and you're in me
I'm in you and you're in me
I'm in you and you're in me

I'm in you and you're in me
I'm in you and you're in me
I'm in you and you're in me
I'm in you and you're in me

Come
Intensify

Come
Open up our hearts
And our mi-inds
Mi-i-inds

All Fly Like Eagles

[Verse 1]
Em
Fly like an eagle
D
fly so high
Em
Circling the universe
   D
on wings of pure light

[Chorus]
Em
Hey witchi thai thai
D
witchi thai yo
Em
Hey witchi thai thai
D
witchi thai yo

[Verse 2]
Em
We all fly like eagles
D
fly so high
Em
Circling the universe
   D
on wings of pure love

[Chorus]
Em
Hey witchi thai thai
D
witchi thai yo
Em
Hey witchi thai thai
D
witchi thai yo

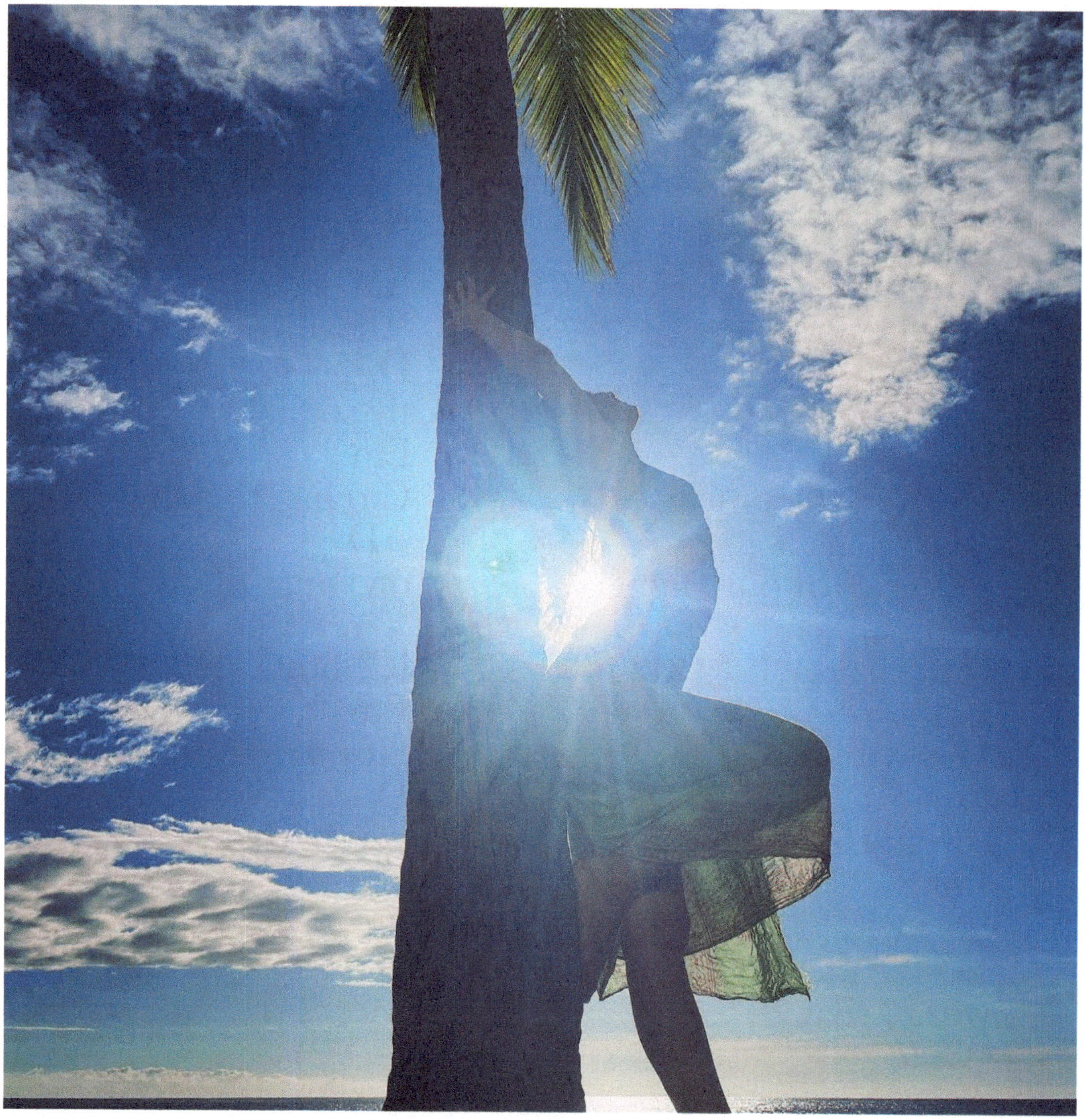

Come, Come Whoever You Are
Based on a Poem by Rumi

[Verse]
   Am   Fmaj7
Come, come, whoever you are
 G   G6   C   Em7
wanderer, worshiper, lover of leaving
   Am   Fmaj7
come, come whoever you are
 G   G6   C   Em7
this isn't a caravan of despair
 Dm   E7
And it doesn't matter if you've broken your vows
 C   D7   Fmaj7
a thousand times before and yet again
     G   C
come again come, and yet again come.

[Chorus]
 G   F
come again come
 G   F
come again come
 G   F
come again come
 G   F C
come again come
  X

All I Ask of You
(Sufi)

G D Em C G D G

All I ask of you is forever
to remember me
as loving you (2x)

G C D Em C D G D

Ishq'allah Mabud Layla
Ishq'allah Mabud Layla

Friends forever yes we are,
your Love lives in my heart (2x)

[This is a Sufi song. The Sufis are mystics from the Islamic tradition,
one of the most famous of whom was the mystical poet Rumi.
The Arabic translates as: God is Love, Lover, & Beloved]

Made for Love

Em -> Am

Love Love Love Love

People we are made for Love

To love each other as ourselves

For we are one

We are one

*

One One One One

Children there is only one

One Spirit in everyone

& It's name is

Love
*
Love Love Love Love...

Everybody Feels Happy Inside

    G   C
Everybody feels happy inside
   G   C
They just don't know it yet
   G   C
Everyone's in love with life
    G   C
It's the best kept secret
   G   C
'Cause we are made of
    G   C
the stuff of the stars
   G   C
and we dance to the rhythm
   G   C
of the beat of our hearts
     D
and we dance
  C   G
until we die and are born again (2x)
REPEAT

Last time: And we dance
And never die & then
THE END

Start the Day With Love

C Am F G

Start the day with love

Spend the day with love

Fill the day with love

End the day with love

Hey Hey!
Yeah here what we say
Every day Every day Everyday
Come what may Come what may
Come what may!

Start the day with love

Spend the day with love

Fill the day with love

End the day with love

Love is the Answer

What was the question?

The Way of the Heart

Am G F G Am

Let the way of the heart
Let the way of the heart
Let the way of the heart
Shine through

Love
Upon Love
Upon Love -
All hearts are beating as one

Light
Upon Light
Upon Light

Shining as bright as the sun!

Let the way of the heart...

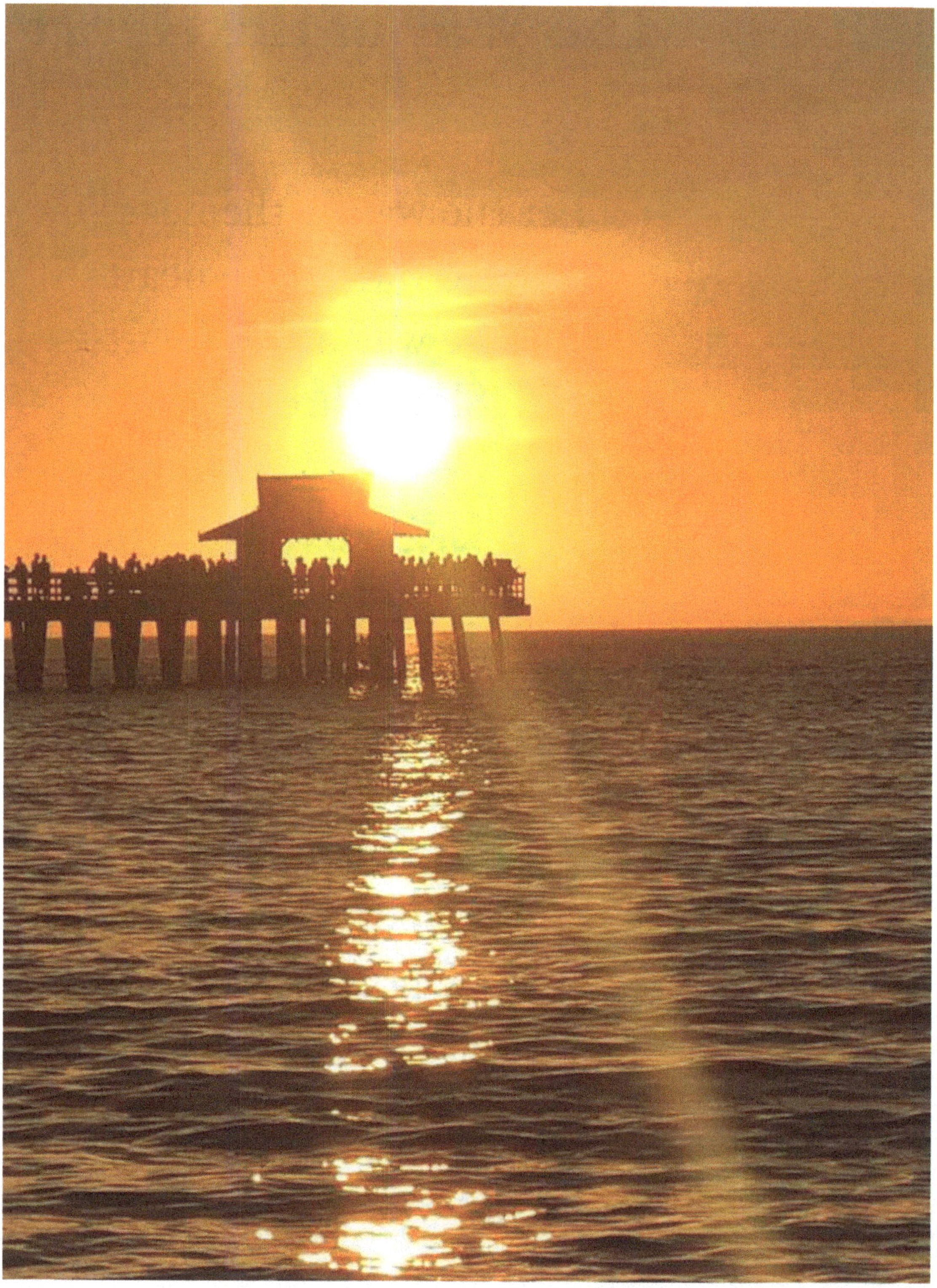

Earth My Body

Am
earth my body
G
water my blood
Am
air my breath
G
fire my spirit—

Am
earth my body
G
water my blood
Am
air my breath
G
fire my spirit—

Am
earth my body
G
water my blood
Am
air my breath
G
fire my spirit—

Peace of the river

C G Am F Dm G C

Peace I ask of thee o river,
peace, peace, peace.
When I learn to live serenely,
cares will cease.
From the hills I gather courage,
visions of the days to be,
Strength to lead and faith to follow,
all is given unto me.
Peace I ask of thee o river,
peace, peace, peace.

Mother I Feel You

Mother I feel you under my feet,
Mother I hear your heartbeat
Mother I feel you under my feet,
Mother I hear your heartbeat

heya heya heya yah heya heya ho
heya heya heya heya heya ho

Mother I hear you in the River song,
eternal waters flowing on and on.
Mother I hear you in the River song,
eternal waters flowing on and on

heya heya heya yah heya heya ho
heya heya heya heya heya ho

Father I see you when the Eagle flies,
Light of the Spirit going to take us higher.
Father I see you when the Eagle flies,
Light of the Spirit going to take us higher.

heya heya heya yah heya heya ho
heya heya heya heya heya ho

Mother I feel you under my feet,
Mother I hear your heartbeat
Mother I feel you under my feet,
Mother I hear your heartbeat

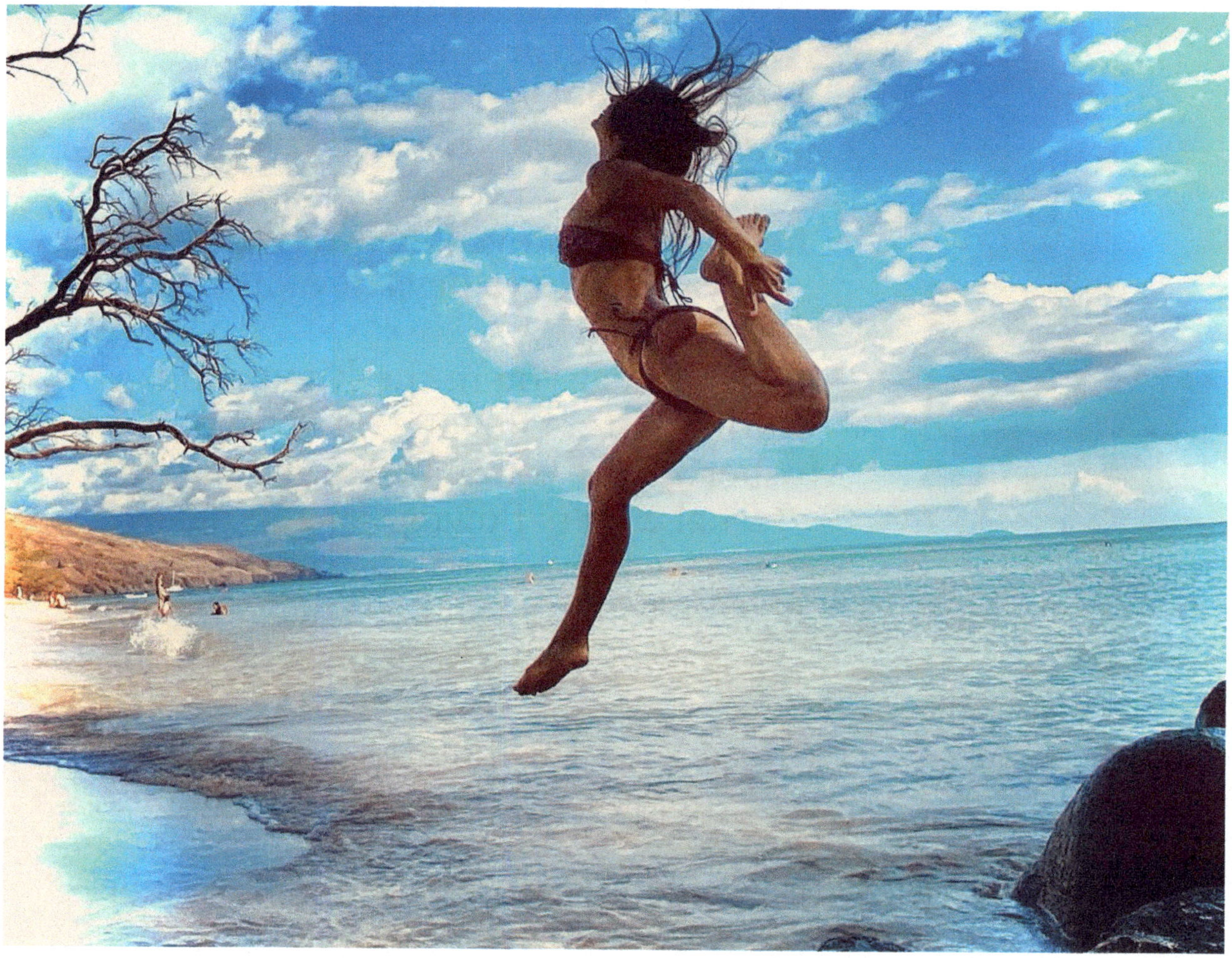

Wishi Ta
(Native American)

Wishi Ta doo-ee-ah–doo-ee-ah–doo-ee-ah

Wishi Ta doo-ee-ah–doo-ee-ah–doo-ay-eh

Washa te-nay-ya – heya – heya

Washa te-nay-ya – hey-ai –ey
X 2

Originally from Brooke Medicine Eagle – a Native American singer/teacher/healer from the Crow Tribe

She refers to this chant as a river song which calls upon two different moods of water – the gentle flowing eddies and also the swift, swirling, white water

Long Time Sun
(3HO Kundalini Yoga)

D A G D

May the Long Time Sun Shine Upon You

All Love Surround You

& The Pure Light Within You

Guide Your Way On (Home)

Shine On

[This song is actually originally from the end of a song by the Scottish rock band, the Incredible String Band, recorded in the Sixties.
The song is called "The Hangman's Beautiful Daughter."]

GOSPEL SONGS

Peace Like A River
(Gospel)

I've got peace like a river, I've got peace like a river,

I've got peace like a river in my soul (repeat)

I've got love like an ocean, I've got love like an ocean,

I've got love like an ocean in my soul (repeat)

I've got joy like a fountain, I've got joy like a fountain

I've got joy like a fountain in my soul. (repeat)

I've got peace like a river

I've got love like an ocean

I've got joy like a fountain in my soul (repeat)

I've got peace like a river, I've got peace like a river,

I've got peace like a river in my soul (repeat)

This Little Light of Mine
(Gospel)

This little light of mine
I'm gonna let it shine

This little light of mine
I'm gonna let it shine

This little light of mine
I'm gonna let it shine

Let it shine, let it shine, let it shine

Everywhere I go, I'm gonna let it shine (3x)

Let it shine (3x)

Shines in you and it shines in me
Let's all let it shine (3x)

All around the world
We gonna let it shine (3x)

This little light of mine...

Amazing Grace
(Christian, traditional)

Amazing grace! How sweet the sound
That saved a wretch like me!
I once was lost, but now am found;
Was blind, but now I see.

'Twas grace that taught my heart to fear,
And grace my fears relieved;
How precious did that grace appear
The hour I first believed.

Through many dangers, toils and snares,
I have already come;
'Tis grace hath brought me safe thus far,
And grace will lead me home.

When we've been there ten thousand years,
Bright shining as the sun,
We've no less days to sing God's praise
Than when we'd first begun.

We Shall Overcome

We shall overcome,

We shall overcome We shall overcome, some day.

Oh, deep in my heart,
I do believe
We shall overcome, some day.

We'll walk hand in hand,
We'll walk hand in hand,
We'll walk hand in hand, some day.

Oh, deep in my heart...

We shall live in peace,
We shall live in peace,
We <u>shall</u> live in peace, some day.

Oh, deep in my heart....

We shall all be free,

We shall all be free,
We shall all be free, some day.

Oh, deep in my heart....

We are not afraid,
We are not afraid,
We are not afraid, TODAY

Oh, deep in my heart....

We shall overcome,
We shall overcome,
We shall overcome, some day.

Oh, deep in my heart....
I do believe
We <u>shall</u> overcome, some day.

Study War No More

I'm gonna lay down my sword and shield

Down by the riverside and study war no more

Down by the riverside I'm gonna lay my burden down

Down by the riverside I'm gonna lay my burden down

Down by the riverside I'm gonna lay my burden down

And I'll study war no more

I ain't gonna study war no more, study war no more

I ain't gonna study war no more

I ain't gonna study war no more, study war no more

I ain't gonna study war no more

Down by the riverside I'm gonna walk with the Prince of Peace

Down by the riverside I'm gonna walk with the Prince of Peace, Hallelujah

Down by the riverside I'm gonna walk with the Prince of Peace

And I'll study war no more

I ain't gonna study war no more, study war no more

I ain't gonna study war no more

I ain't gonna study war no more, study war no more

I ain't gonna study war no more

I'm gonna beat my sword into a cloud down by the riverside

I'm gonna beat my sword into a cloud down by the riverside, yes it is

Beat my sword into a cloud down by the riverside

And I'll study war no more

I ain't gonna study war no more, study war no more

I ain't gonna study war no more

I ain't gonna study war no more, study war no more

I ain't gonna study war no more

Go Down, Moses

Go down Moses
Way down in Egypt land
Tell all pharaoes to
Let my people go!

When Israel was in Egypt land
Let my people go!

Oppressed so hard they could not stand
Let my people go!

So the God said: go down, Moses
Way down in Egypt land
Tell all pharaoes to
Let my people go!

So moses went to Egypt land
Let my people go!

He made all pharaoes understand
Let my people go!
Yes the lord said: go down, Moses
Way down in Egypt land
Tell all pharaoes to
Let my people go!

Thus spoke the lord, bold Moses said:
-let my people go!
if not I'll smite, your firstborn's dead
-let my people go!

God-the lord said : go down, Moses
Way down in Egypt land
Tell all pharaoes to
Let my people go!

Tell all pharaoes
To let my people go

Let Your Light Shine On Me
Blind Willie Johnson

[Chorus]
Let it shine on me, let it shine on me
Oh, let Your light from the lighthouse shine on me
Let it shine on me, let it shine on me
Oh, let Your light from the lighthouse shine on

[Verse 1]
My Lord, he's done just what he said
Let Your light from the lighthouse shine on me
Heal the sick and rise the dead
Let Your light from the lighthouse shine on...

[Chorus]
Oh, let it shine on, well, let it shine on
Let Your light from the lighthouse shine on me
Shine on, oh, let it shine on
Let Your light from the lighthouse shine on...

[Verse 2]
I know I've got religion and I ain't ashamed
Let Your light from the lighthouse shine on me
Angels in Heaven, done wrote my name
Let Your light from the lighthouse shine on...

[Chorus]
Oh, let it shine on, oh, let it shine on
Let Your light from the lighthouse shine on me
Shine on well, let it shine on
Let Your light from the lighthouse shine on...

Kum Ba Yah

Kum ba yah, my lord, Kum ba yah!
Kum ba yah, my lord, Kum ba yah!
Kum ba yah, my lord, Kum ba yah.
O Lord, Kum ba yah

Someone's crying, Lord, Kum ba yah!
Someone's crying, Lord, Kum ba yah!
Someone's crying, Lord, Kum ba yah!
O Lord, Kum ba yah

Someone's singing, Lord, Kum ba yah!
Someone's singing, Lord, Kum ba yah!
Someone's singing, Lord, Kum ba yah!
O Lord, Kum ba yah

Someone's praying, Lord, Kum ba yah!
Someone's praying, Lord, Kum ba yah!
Someone's praying, Lord, Kum ba yah!
O Lord, Kum ba yah

I'll Fly Away

[Verse 1]

G   G7   C   G
Some glad morning when this life is o'er, I'll fly away
G   D7   G
To a home on God's celestial shore, I'll fly away

[Chorus]

G   G7   C   G
I'll fly away, O glory, I'll fly away
G   C G   D7   G
When I die, hallelujah, by and by I'll fly away

[Verse 2]

G   G7   C   G
When the shadows of this life have grown, I'll fly away
G   D7   G
Like a bird from prison bars has flown, I'll fly away

[Chorus]

G   G7   C   G
I'll fly away, O glory, I'll fly away
G   C G   D7   G
When I die, hallelujah, by and by I'll fly away

[Verse 3]

G   G7   C   G
Oh how glad and happy when we meet, I'll fly away
G   D7   G
No more cold iron shackles on my feet, I'll fly away

[Chorus]

G   G7   C   G
I'll fly away, O glory, I'll fly away
G   C G   D7   G
When I die, hallelujah, by and by I'll fly away

[Verse 4]

G   G7   C   G
Just a few more weary days, and then, I'll fly away
G   D7   G
To a land where joys shall never end, I'll fly away

[Chorus]

G   G7   C   G
I'll fly away, O glory, I'll fly away
G   C G   D7   G
When I die, hallelujah, by and by I'll fly away
X

Glory, Glory, Hallelujah

Glory, glory, hallelujah!
Since I laid my burdens down. Glory, glory, hallelujah!

Since I laid my burdens down! I feel better, so much better

Since I laid my burdens down. I feel better, so much better

Since I laid my burdens down! Friends don't treat me like they used to

Since I laid my burdens down. Friends don't treat me like they used to

Since I laid my burdens down! I'm goin' home to be with Jesus

Since I laid my burdens down. I'm goin' home to be with Jesus

Since I laid my burdens down! I won't treat you like I used to

Since I laid my burdens down. I won't treat you like I used to

Since I laid my burdens down! Burdens down, Lord, burdens down

Since I laid my burdens down. Burdens down, Lord, burdens down

Since I laid my burdens down! Glory, glory, hallelujah!

Since I laid my burdens down. Glory, glory, hallelujah!

Since I laid my burdens down

Rise And Shine

Chorus:
Rise and shine and give God
your glory, glory!
Rise and shine and give God
your glory, glory!
Rise and shine and (clap once)
give God your glory, glory!
(Raise hands to shoulder level
and sway back and forth.)
Children of the Lord.

The Lord said to Noah,
"There's gonna be a floody,
floody."
Lord said to Noah, "There's
gonna be a floody, floody."
"Get those children (clap once)
out of the muddy, muddy!"
Children of the Lord.

So Noah, he built him, he built
him an arky, arky.
Noah, he built him, he built
him an arky, arky.
Made it out of (clap once)
hickory barky, barky.
Children of the Lord.

The animals, they came on,
they came on by twosies,
twosies.
The animals, they came on,
they came on by twosies,
twosies.
Elephants and (clap once)
kangaroosies, roosies.
Children of the Lord.

Chorus

It rained, and poured, for forty
daysies, daysies.
Rained, and poured, for forty
daysies, daysies.
Nearly drove those (clap once)
animals crazy, crazy.
Children of the Lord.

The sun came out and dried up
the landy, landy.
Sun came out and dried up the
landy, landy.
Everything was (clap once) fine
and dandy, dandy.
Children of the Lord.

Now that is the end, the end of
my story, story.
That is the end, the end of my
story, story.
Everything is (clap once) hunky
dory, dory.
Children of the Lord.

Chorus

When the Saints Go Marching In

Traditional

    C
O when the saints go marchin' in,
    G7
O when the saints go marchin' in,
  C7   F
Lord, I want to be in that number
    C   G7 C
When the saints go marchin' in.

[Verse 2]
(same chords)

O when the sun refuse to shine,
O when the sun refuse to shine,
Lord, I want to be in that number
When the sun refuse to shine.

[Verse 3]
(same chords)

O when the moon goes down in blood,
O when the moon goes down in blood,
Lord, I want to be in that number
When the moon goes down in blood.

[Verse 4]
(same chords)

O when the stars have disappeared,
O when the stars have disappeared,
Lord, I want to be in that number
When the stars have disappeared,

[Verse 5]
(same chords)

O when they crown Him Lord of all,
O when they crown Him Lord of all,
Lord, I want to be in that number
When they crown Him Lord of all.

[Verse 6]
(same chords)

O when the day of judgement comes,
O when the day of judgement comes,
Lord, I want to be in that number
When the day of judgement comes.

The Lion of Judah

E B7 A E
The Lion of Judah shall break every chain (3x)
Give us Jah Victory Again & Again

That Conquering Lion shall break every chain (3x)
Give us Jah Victory again & again

The Lion of Judah shall break every chain (3x)
Give us Jah Victory Again & Again

Proverbs 28:1: נָסוּ וְאֵין־רֹדֵף רָשָׁע וְצַדִּיקִים כִּכְפִיר יִבְטָח:

The wicked flee when no man pursueth, but the righteous are bold as a lion

The Glory Train

The glory train goes riding by,
    Hallelujah!
A golden streaking in the sky,
A gleam and whistling rising hih,
Above all souls that thought to die,
    Hallelujah!

Do not look up or you might see
An angel standing by the tree,
And see the halo round His head
And scream because you think you're dead.

The glory train will come at last,
    Hallelujah!
With crucifixion as a mast,
A blur of lightnin' ripping past
All things you love that will not last,
    Hallelujah!

Close up your ears or you might hear
The trumpet of the Charioteer,
And feel your heart's song miss a beat
To see His arrow at your feet.

Slow down the glory train for me,
    Hallelujah!
I see my Brother there and He
Is holding out a golden key
To raise my eyes that I might see,
    Hallelujah!

Come down, my Brother, come for me.
What fear has made I would not see.
The door is open. Where You stand
Is holy ground and Heavenland.
I did not understand the song,
    Hallelujah!
I thought to die but now I long
Only to join the risen throng
That rides the stars with You along,
    Hallelujah!

There is no death, and life rides by
Until You stop to raise us high
And touch our eyes and ears, so we
Long deaf and blind, can hear and see,
    Hallelujah!

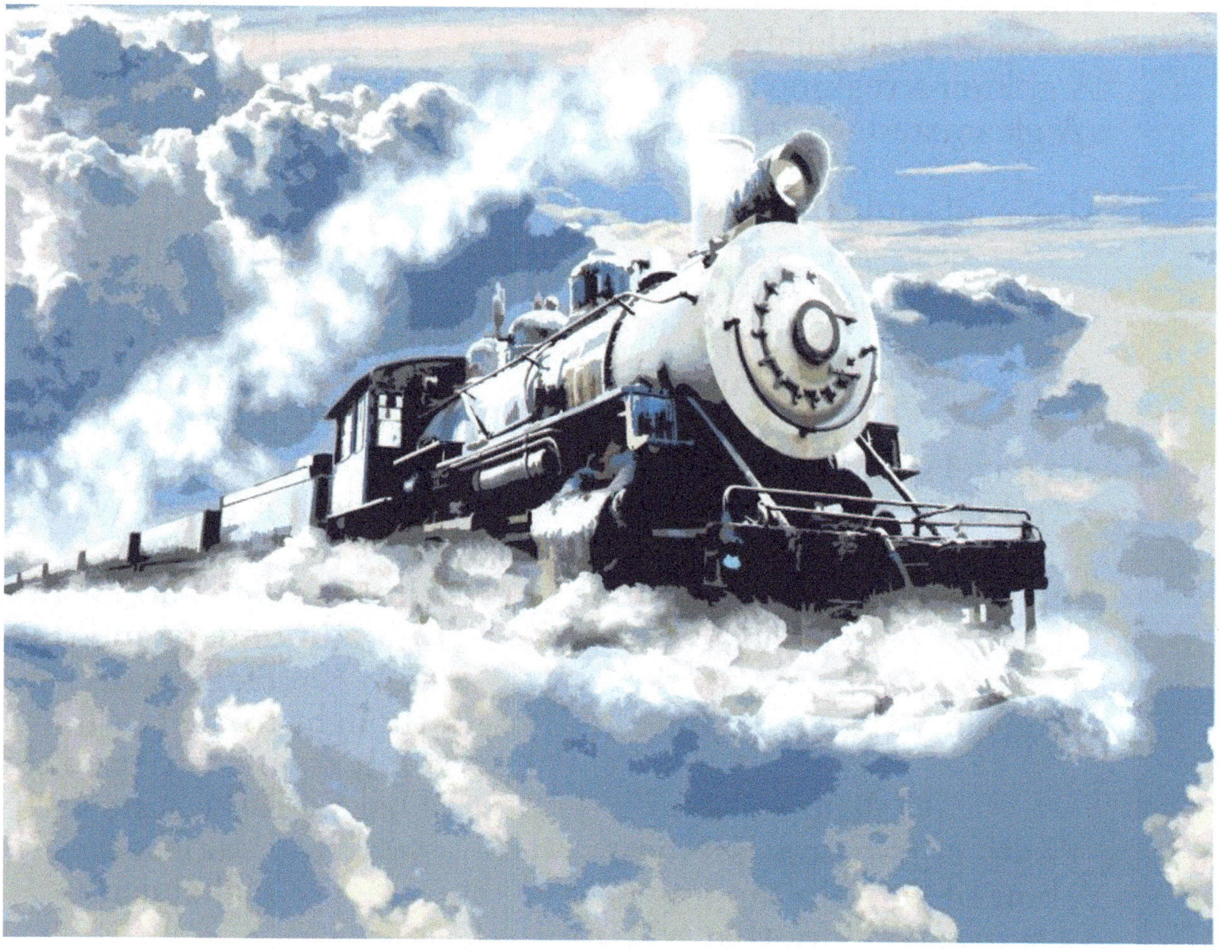

And We Bid You Goodnight

Lay down my dear brothers, lay down and take your rest

Oh, won't you lay your head upon your savior's breast

I love you, oh but <u>Jesus</u> loves you the best

   And we bid you goodnight, goodnight, goodnight

   And we bid you goodnight, goodnight, goodnight

   And we bid you goodnight, goodnight, goodnight

Walking in Jerusalem, just like John

(Bid you goodnight, goodnight, goodnight)

I <u>remember</u> right well, I <u>remember</u> right well

(Bid you goodnight, goodnight, goodnight)

His rod and his <u>staff</u> shall <u>comfort</u> me

(Bid you goodnight, goodnight, goodnight)

Tell "A" for the ark, that <u>wonderful</u> boat

(Bid you goodnight, goodnight, goodnight)

Tell "B" for the <u>beast</u> at the <u>ending</u> of the wood

(Bid you goodnight, goodnight, goodnight)

You know, it ate all the <u>children</u> that <u>would</u> not be good

(Bid you goodnight, goodnight, goodnight)

Walking in the <u>valley</u> in the <u>shadow</u> of death

(Bid you goodnight, goodnight, goodnight)

Lay down my dear brothers, lay down and take your rest

Oh, won't you lay your head upon your savior's breast

I love you, oh but <u>Jesus</u> loves you the best

   And we bid you goodnight, goodnight, goodnight

   And we bid you goodnight, goodnight, goodnight

FOLK SONGS

This Land Is Your Land

[D]This land is [G]your land, this land is [D]my land,
From Calif[A7]ornia to the New York [D]Island,
From the Redwood F[G]orests to the Gulf Stream wa[D]ters;
[A7]This land was made for you and [D]me.

As I was walking that ribbon of highway,
I looked above me, there in the skyway,
I saw below me, the Golden Valley;
This land was made for you and me.

I roamed and rambled, and followed my footsteps
Through the sparkling sands of her diamond deserts,
And all around me this voice kept saying,
"This land was made for you and me."

As the Sun was shining, and I was strolling
Through the wheat fields waving and the dust clouds rolling,
I could feel inside me and see all around me,
This land was made for you and me.

Guantanamera

    C   D7
Guantanamera,
  G   D7
guajira Guantanamera
  G   C D7
Guantanamera,
  G   C D7
guajira Guantanamera

  G   C   D7
Yo soy un hombre sincero
  G   C   D7
De donde crece la palma.
  G   C   D7
Yo soy un hombre sincero
  G   C   D7
De donde crece la palma
  G   C   D7
Y antes de morirme quiero
  G   C D7
Echar mis versos del alma.

    Chorus

  G   C   D7
Mi verso es de un verde claro
  G   C   D7
Y de un carmín encendido.
  G   C   D7
Mi verso es de un verde claro
  G   C   D7
Y de un carmín encendido.
  G   C   D7
Mi verso es un ciervo herido
  G   C D7
Que busca en el monte amparo.

    Chorus

  G   C   D7
Con los pobres de la tierra
  G   C   D7
Quiero yo mi suerte echar.
  G   C   D7
Con los pobres de la tierra
  G   C   D7
Quiero yo mi suerte echar.
  G   C   D7
Un arroyo de la tierra
  G   C   D7
Me complace más que el mar.

    Chorus

Blowin' in the Wind
(Robert Zimmerman)
D G A

How many <u>roads</u> must a man walk down
Before you call him a man
How many seas must a <u>white</u> dove sail
Before she <u>sleeps</u> in the sand
Yes, 'n' how many <u>times</u> must the <u>cannon</u> balls fly
Before they're <u>forever</u> banned
The answer, my friend, is blowin' in the wind
The <u>answer</u> is blowin' in the wind

Yes, 'n' how many <u>years</u> can a <u>mountain</u> exist
Before it's <u>washed</u> to the sea
Yes, 'n' how many <u>years</u> can some <u>people</u> exist
Before they're <u>allowed</u> to be free
Yes, 'n' how many <u>times</u> can a man turn his head
And <u>pretend</u> that he just doesn't see
The answer, my friend, is blowin' in the wind
The <u>answer</u> is blowin' in the wind

Yes, 'n' how many <u>times</u> must a man look up
Before he can see the sky
Yes, 'n' how many ears must one man have
Before he can hear <u>people</u> cry
Yes, 'n' how many <u>deaths</u> will it take till he knows
That too many <u>people</u> have died
The answer, my friend, is blowin' in the wind
The <u>answer</u> is blowin' in the wind

Turn! Turn! Turn! (To Everything There Is a Season)

To everything (turn, turn, turn)
There is a season (turn, turn, turn)
And a time for every purpose, under heaven

A time to be born, a time to die
A time to plant, a time to reap
A time to kill, a time to heal
A time to laugh, a time to weep

To everything (turn, turn, turn)
There is a season (turn, turn, turn)
And a time for every purpose, under heaven

A time to build up, a time to break down
A time to dance, a time to mourn
A time to cast away stones, a time to gather stones together

To everything (turn, turn, turn)
There is a season (turn, turn, turn)
And a time for every purpose, under heaven

A time of love, a time of hate
A time of war, a time of peace
A time you may embrace, a time to refrain from embracing

To everything (turn, turn, turn)
There is a season (turn, turn, turn)
And a time for every purpose, under heaven

A time to gain, a time to lose
A time to rend, a time to sew
A time to love, a time to hate
A time for peace, I swear its not too late

To everything (turn, turn, turn)
There is a season (turn, turn, turn)
And a time for every purpose, under heaven

A time to be born, a time to die
A time to plant, a time to reap
A time to kill, a time to heal
A time to laugh, a time to weep

To everything (turn, turn, turn)
There is a season (turn, turn, turn)
And a time for every purpose, under heaven

A time to build up, a time to break down
A time to dance, a time to mourn
A time to cast away stones, a time to gather stones together

To everything (turn, turn, turn)
There is a season (turn, turn, turn)
And a time for every purpose, under heaven

A time of love, a time of hate
A time of war, a time of peace
A time you may embrace, a time to refrain from embracing

To everything (turn, turn, turn)
There is a season (turn, turn, turn)
And a time for every purpose, under heaven

A time to gain, a time to lose
A time to rend, a time to sew
A time to love, a time to hate
A time for peace, I swear its not too late

Hava Nagila

    E   Am   E
Hava nagila, hava nagila, hava nagila v'nis-m'cha
(Let us rejoice and jubilate!)

      G   Am   E
Hava nagila, hava nagila, v'nis-m'cha

           Dm
Hava n'ra-n'na, hava n'ra-n'na, hava n'ra-n'na
      E
v'nis-m'cha   (let us sing and rejoice)
Dm
Hava n'ra-n'na, hava n'ra-n'na, hava n'ra-n'na
      E
v-nis-m'cha
Am
U-ru uru a-chim, u-ru a-chim

U-ru a-chim b'lev sa-may-ach
(Awake brothers with joyful hearts)

u-ru A-chim B-lev sa-may-ach
      Dm
U-ru a-chim b'lev sa-may-ach
  E   Am
U-ru a-chim b'lev sa-may-ach

Hava nagila, hava nagila, hava nagila v'nis-m'cha

Hava nagila, hava nagila, hava nagila v'nis-m'cha\

Paranuê
C F G C

Vou dizer minha mulher, Paraná
(I'm going to tell my wife)
Capoeira me venceu, Paraná
(Capoeira saved me)
Paranauê, paranauê, Paraná
Paranauê, paranauê, Paraná
Vou me embora pra favela, Paraná
(I'm going now to the favela)
Como já disse que vou, Paraná (As I
already said I'd go)

Paranauê, paranauê, Paraná
Paranauê, paranauê, Paraná
E desvera que o morro, Paraná (And
deserves that the hill)
Se mudou para cidade, Paraná
(Changes for the City)

Paranauê, paranauê, Paraná
Paranauê, paranauê, Paraná
Vou me embora dessa terra, Paraná
(I go now from this land)
Como já disse que vou, Paraná (As I
already said I'll go)

Paranauê, paranauê, Paraná
Paranauê, paranauê, Paraná
Eu aqui não sou querido, Paraná
(Here I am not loved)
Mas na minha terra eu sou, Paraná
(But in my land I am)

Paranauê, paranauê, Paraná
Paranauê, paranauê, Paraná
Cantando com alegria, Paraná
(Singing with joy)
Mocidade es que mata, Paraná
(Youth is what kills)

Paranauê, paranauê, Paraná
Paranauê, paranauê, Paraná
O enfeite de uma mesa, Paraná (The
decoration of a table)
É um garfo e uma colher, Paraná (Is
a fork and a spoon)

Paranauê, paranauê, Paraná
Paranauê, paranauê, Paraná
O enfeite de uma cama, Paraná (The
decoration of a bed)
É um homem e uma mulher, Paraná
(Is a man and a woman)

Paranauê, paranauê, Paraná
Paranauê, paranauê, Paraná
Mulher pra ser bonita, Paraná (A
woman, to be beautiful)
Não precisa se pintar, Paraná
(Doesn't need make up)

Paranauê, paranauê, Paraná
Paranauê, paranauê, Paraná

ושאבתם מים בששו
Ushavtem Mayim

ממעייני הישועה
ושאבתם מים בששון
ממעייני הישועה.
מים, מים, מים מים
הוי מים בששון.
מים, מים, מים, מים,
הוי מים בששון

Ushavtem maim besason
Mima'ayanei hayeshua
Ushavtem maim besason
Mima'ayanei hayeshua
Maim, maim, maim, maim
Hey maim besason
Maim, maim, maim, maim
Hey maim besason

Let us draw water joyfully
from the wellsprings of Salvation!

The Water Is Wide

    C   G   C G
The water is wide, I can't cross o'er
D Em C   D
Nor do I have light wings to fly
Bm   Em C
Build me a boat that can carry two
D D_7 G
And both shall row, my love and I

     C   G   C G
A ship there is and sails the sea
D Em C   D
She's loaded deep, as deep can be
Bm   Em C
But not so deep as the love I'm in
D D_7 G
And I know not how, I sink or swim

    G   C G Em C D
D Bm Em C D D_7 G

    C   G   C G
When love is young and love is fine
D Em C   D
It's like a gem when first it's new
Bm   Em C
But love grows old and waxes cold
D D_7 G
And fades away like the morning dew

    C   G   C G
The water is wide, I can't cross o'er
D Em C   D
Nor do I have light wings to fly
Bm   Em C
Build me a boat that can carry two
D D_7 G C G
And both shall row, my love and I_____

DEVOTIONAL SONGS

I Am As God Created Me
(based on A Course in Miracles)

D C G

I am still as God created me,

In the light in the love in the glory

In the light, In the love, in the glory, I am

In the light, in the love, in the glory, I am.

I am still as God created me,

In the light in the love in the glory x 2

In the light, in the light, in the love, in the glory.

In the light, in the love, in the glory,
I am

The Prayer of Saint Francis

Lord make me an instrument of your peace
Where there is hatred let me sow love
Where there is injury, pardon
Where there is doubt, faith
Where there is despair, hope
Where there is darkness, light
And where there is sadness, joy

O divine master grant that I may
not so much seek to be consoled as to console
to be understood as to understand
To be loved as to love
For it is in giving that we receive
it is in pardoning that we are pardoned
And it's in dying that we are born to eternal life

Amen

Love, Serve, Remember
Words by Paramhansa Yogananda, Music by John Astin

(Capo 2) E B A E B A

Why have you come to earth, do you remember?

E B A E B A Why have you taken birth, why have you come?

E B A To love, serve and remember,

E B A To love, serve and remember

E to love In This Circle

Only Here For Love

Rickie Byars & Michael Beckwith

Am E7

I release & I let go

I let spirit run my life

And my heart is open wide

I'm only here for love

No more struggle no more strife
With my faith I see the light
I am free in the spare
Yes, I'm only here for God

Let Go, Let God....

Gesher Tsar Me'od

Rabbi Nachman of Breslov

Kol ha'olam kulo
Gesher tzar me'od

Gesher tzar me'od

Gesher tzar me'od

Veha'ikar lo lifached k'lal.

All the entire world
is a very narrow bridge

a very narrow bridge

a very narrow bridge

& the main thing, the main thing
is not to be afraid

& the main thing, the main thing
Is not to fear at all

The Greatest Commandment

Shalom

V'ahafta et Adonai
B'col levavcha
B'col nafshekha
Y'v'col me'odekha

V'reyekha camokha
V'reyekha camokha
V'reyekha camokha

And you shall love the Lord thy God
With all thy heart
With all thy soul
& with all thy might

& thy neighbor as thyself
& thy neighbor as thyself
& thy neighbor as thyself

& thy neighbor as thyself
& thy neighbor as thyself
For thy neighbor is thyself

Shalom

Hinei Mah Tov
(Hebrew, from the Book of Psalms)

Hi-nei mah tov u – mah na- im

She-vet a-chim gam ya – chad.

How good and pleasant it is for
everyone to commune
together as one.

(Or, how good & wonderful it is
for brethren to
be together!)

Little Drummer Boy

Come thy told me
Pa rum pum pum-pum
A newborn King to see
Pa rum pum pum-pum
Our finest gifts we bring
Pa rum pum pum-pum
To lay before the king
Pa rum pum pum-pum
Rum pum pum-pum
Rum pum pum-pum
So to honor Him
Pa rum pum pum-pum
When we come

Little baby
Pa rum pum pum-pum
I am a poor boy too
Pa rum pum pum-pum
I have no gift to bring
Pa rum pum pum-pum
That's fit to give our King
Pa rum pum pum-pum
Rum pum pum-pum
Rum pum pum-pum
Shall I play for you
Pa rum pum pum-pum
On my drum

Mary nodded
Pa rum pum pum-pum
The ox and lamb kept time
Pa rum pum pum-pum
I played my drum for Him
Pa rum pum pum-pum
I played my best for Him

Pa rum pum pum-pum
Rum pum pum-pum
Rum pum pum-pum
Then He smiled at me
Pa rum pum pum-pum
Me and my drum

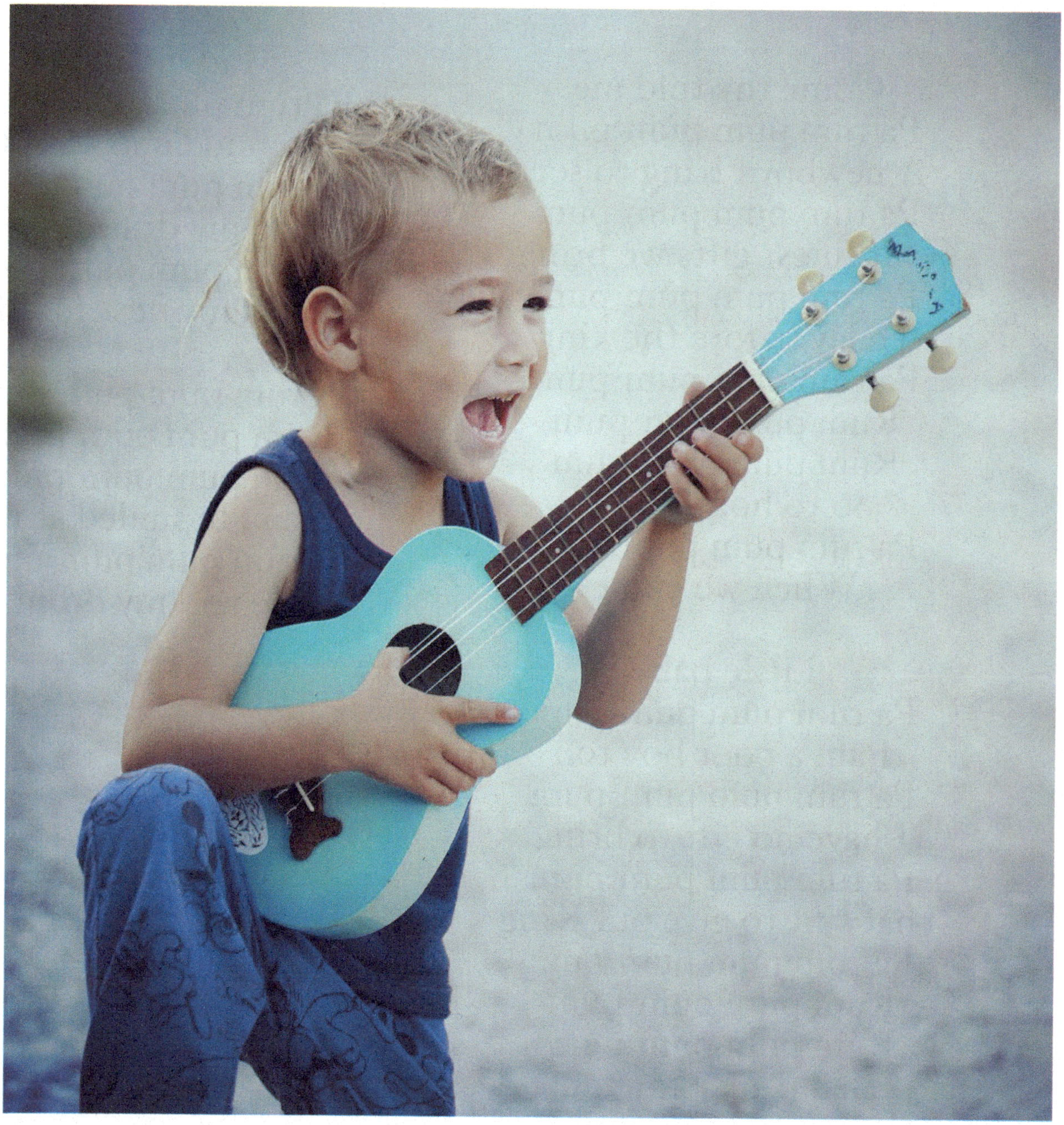

Hodu L'Adonai
(from The Psalms)

*Hodu la'adonai ki tov
ki le'olam chasdo.*

Give Thanks to God
For God is Good
For God's Lovingkindness
Endures Forever

Simple Gifts
(Shaker Song)

Tis' the gift to be simple
tis' the gift to be free
tis' the gift to come down where you ought to be
and when we find ourselves in the place just right
T'will be in the valley of love and delight

When true simplicity is gained
to bow and to bend we shan't be ashamed
to turn, turn will be our delight
til by turning, turning we come 'round right

Tis' the gift to be simple
tis' the gift to be free
tis' the gift to come down where you ought to be
and when we find ourselves in the place just right
t'will be in the valley of love and delight

E'Malama

C Am F C

E'Malama ika heiau

E'Malama ika heiau

E'Malama pono ika heiau E...

Earth & Sky

Sea & Stone

Hold this land in sacredness

Walk In Beauty

May we walk in beauty in a sacred way
May we walk in beauty each & every day
May we sing the glory of the sun
OM Shree Ram Jai Ram Jai Jai Ram

Come on darling, come & take my hand
& together we will walk this land
Let's not even try to understand
Nothing ever seems to go as planned

But we'll walk in beauty in a sacred way
Walk in beauty each & every day
& we'll sing the glory of the sun
OM Shree Ram Jai Ram Jai Jai Ram

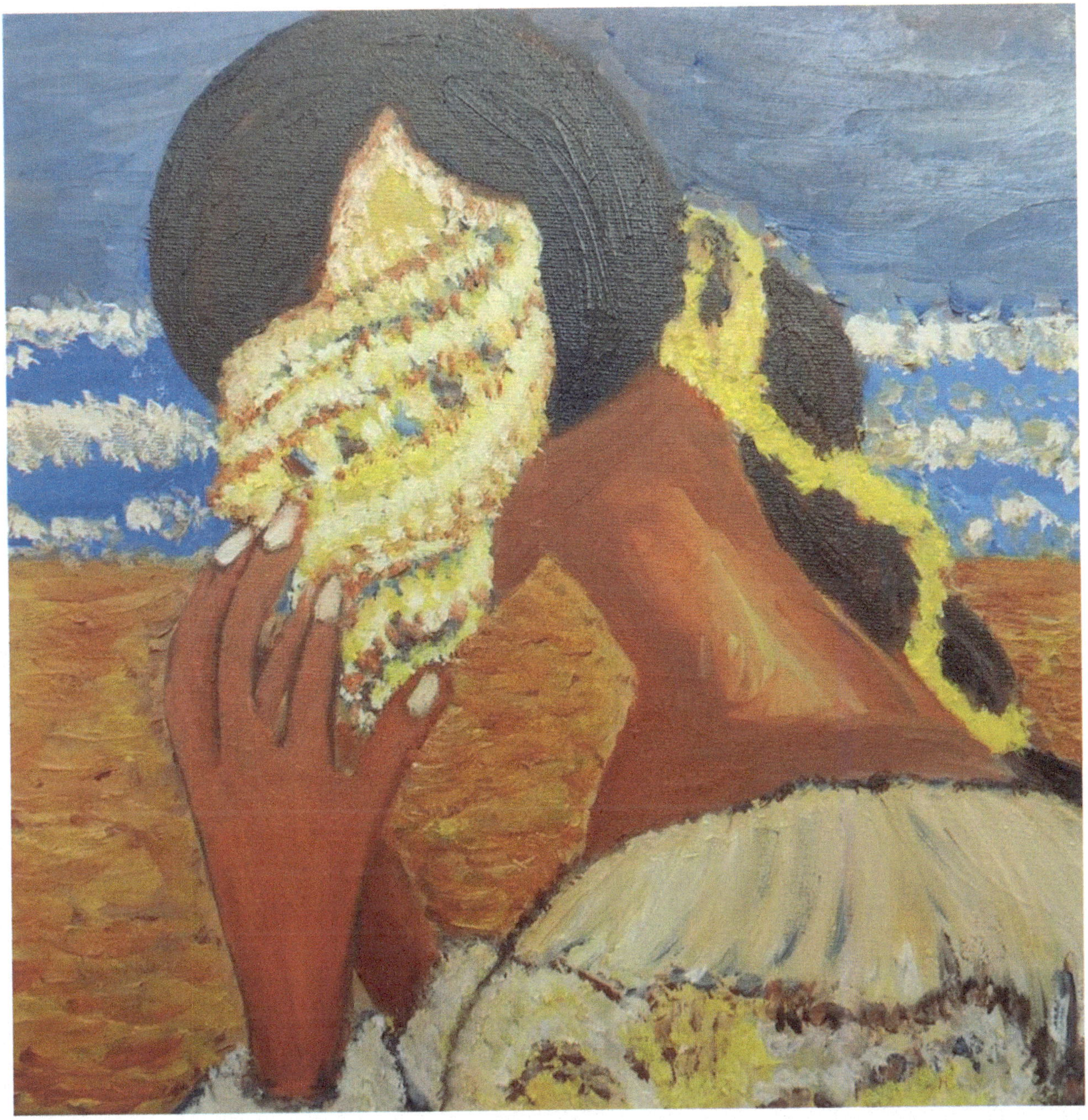

How could anyone?
(Chaina Noll)

     C   F   G
How could anyone ever tell you

  C   G   Am7
You were anything less than beautiful?

   Dm   G
How could anyone ever tell you

  C   G Gm6   C7
You were less than whole?

    F   G
How could anyone fail to notice

     C   G Am7
That your loving is a miracle?

F   G   C
How deeply you're connected to my soul.

La Promesa
(Shimshai)

Cuando todo que tenemos
Es todo que necesitamos
Y el amor de Dios
Siempre estará

Para hacer su trabajo
Y vivir con la paz
Que la promesa del cielo
Esté contigo
Que la promesa del cielo
Esté contigo
Que la promesa del cielo
Esté contigo
Que la promesa del cielo
Esté esté contigo

For when all we have
Is all we need
And the love of the Lord
Will forever be

For to do thy work
And to live in peace
That the promise of heaven
May be with thee
That the promise of heaven
May be with thee

Altar of Love

    G   Cmaj7   G
All that I am, I offer at the Altar of love

    G   Cmaj7   G
All that I am, I offer at the Altar of love

    Em D Cmaj7 G
In sweet surrender

    Em D Cmaj7 G
In sweet surrender

We All Come from the Goddess

Em – 7th fret 5th string
Bm – 7th Fret 6th string
D – 5 Fret 5th String

  Em   D
          Em
We all come from the Goddess
Em Bm   D   Em
And to Her we shall return
  Em   D - Em
Like a drop of rain
 Em Bm   D em
Flowing to the ocean

         Em
Isis, Astarte, Diana,
      D
Hecate, Demeter, Kali,
     Em
Inanna

      Em
the goddess is alive

      Em
magick is afoot.

the goddess is alive

  D //   Em
magick is a-foot.

(alternate verses:)
We all come from the Sun God
And to Him we shall return
Like a ray of light
Reaching to eternity
We all come from the one God
And to the One we shall return
Like a breath of air
Released into an endless sky
We all come from the Goddess
And from Her we take our form
Like a spark of fire
Rising from a dancing flam

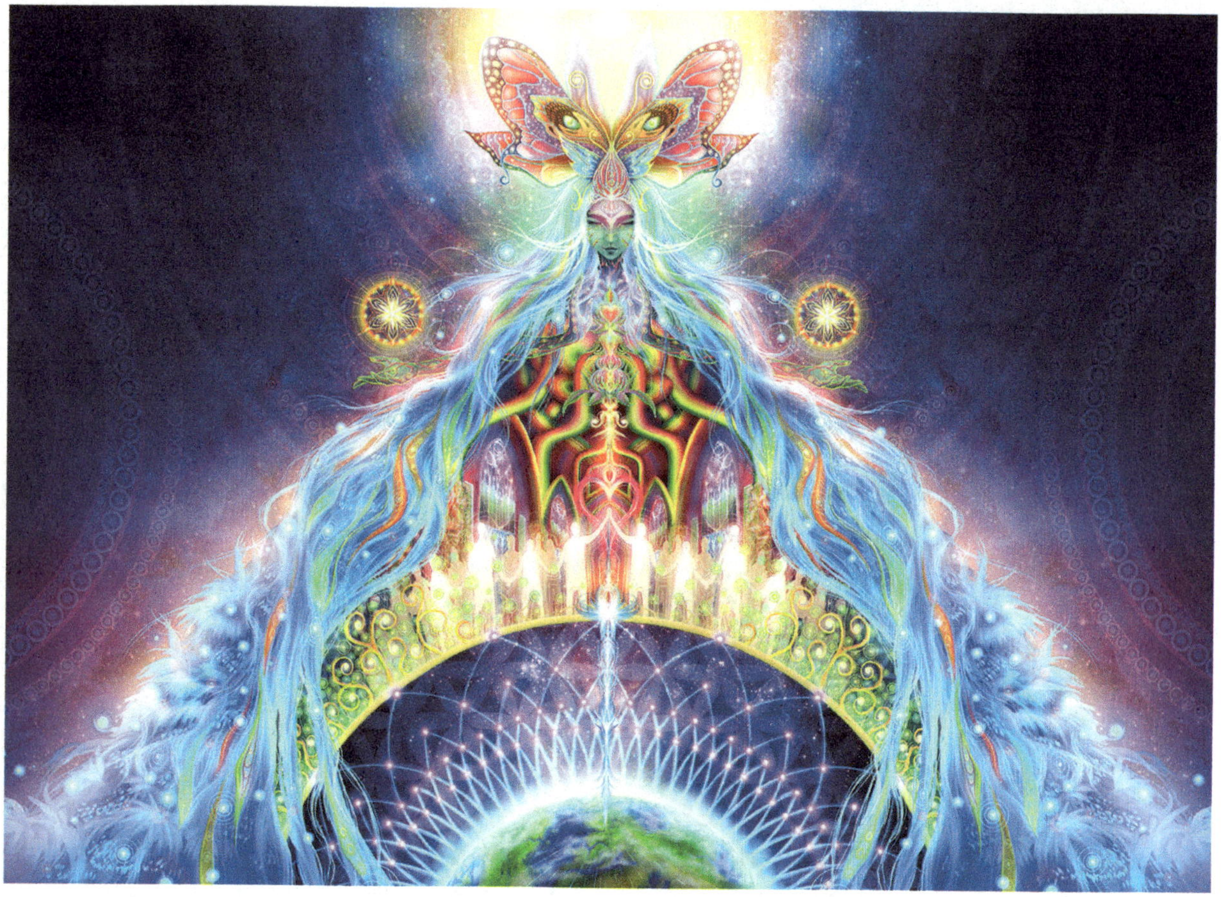

Ode to Joy
(Ode An Die Freude)
From Beethoven's 9th Symphony

   G   D   Em   A
      G D
Freude schöner Götterfunken,
Tochter aus Elysium,

   G   G/F   C   Cm/Eb   G
        D   G
Wir betreten feuertrunken,
Himmlische, dein Heilig - tum!

D   G   D   G   Am   B
     Em   A   D
Deine Zauber binden wieder,
was die Mode streng geteilt.

   G   G7   C   Cm/Eb   G
     Am   D   G
Alle Menschen werden Brüder,
wo dein sanfter Flügel weilt.

   G   D   Em   A
      G   D
Wem der große Wurf
gelungen, eines Freundes
Freund zu sein,

   G   G/F   C   Cm/Eb   G
        D   G
Wer ein holdes Weib errungen,
mische seinen Jubel ein!

D   G   D   G   Am   B
     Em   A   D
Ja, wer auch nur eine Seele sein
nennt auf dem Erdenrund!

   G   G7   C   Cm/Eb   G
     Am   D   G
Und wer's nie gekonnt, der
stehle weinend sich aus diesem
Bund

Ode to Joy
(English translation)

O friends, no more these sounds!
Let us sing more cheerful songs,
more full of joy!
Joy, bright spark of divinity,
Daughter of Elysium,
Fire-inspired we tread
Thy sanctuary.
Thy magic power re-unites
All that custom has divided,
All men become brothers
Under the sway of thy gentle wings.
Whoever has created
An abiding friendship,
Or has won
A true and loving wife,
All who can call at least one soul theirs,
Join in our song of praise;
But any who cannot must creep tearfully
Away from our circle.
All creatures drink of joy
At nature's breast.
Just and unjust
Alike taste of her gift;
She gave us kisses and the fruit of the vine,
A tried friend to the end.
Even the worm can feel contentment,
And the cherub stands before God!
Gladly, like the heavenly bodies
Which He set on their courses
Through the splendor of the firmament;
Thus, brothers, you should run your race,
As a hero going to conquest.
You millions, I embrace you.
This kiss is for all the world!
Brothers, above the starry canopy
There must dwell a loving Father.
Do you fall in worship, you millions?
World, do you know your creator?
Seek him in the heavens;
Above the stars must He dwell.

Forever We Are
(Hanna Leigh)

CFC

Who I Am Is Who I Am
Forever I AM
A Divine Soul (2x)

As we learn and grow
As we learn and grow
We are opening our hearts to the divine flow (2x)

In the Light of This
In the Light of This
All else falls away and there is only bliss (2x)

Who We Are Is Who We Are
Forever We Are A Divine Soul (2x)

Who I Am...

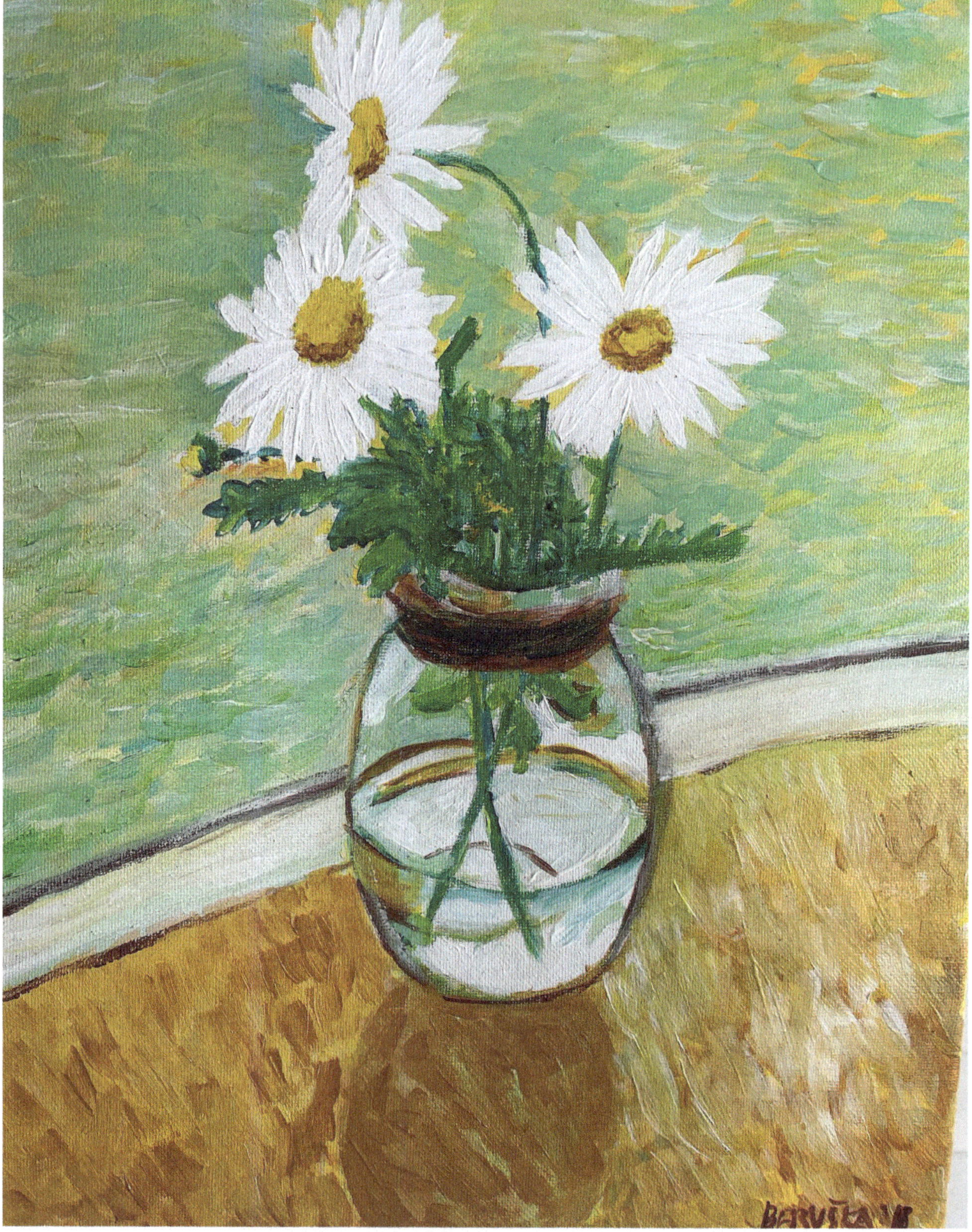

Ani Ve'ata
(Arik Einstein)

Ani ve'ata neshaneh et ha'olam Ani ve'ata az yavo'u kvar kulam Amru et zeh kodem lefanai Zeh lo meshaneh, Ani ve'ata neshaneh et ha'olam Ani ve'ata nenaseh mehatchalah Yiheyl lanu ra ein davar zseh lo nora Amru et zeh kodem lefanai Zeh lo meshaneh, Ani ve'ata neshaneh et ha'olam Ani ve'ata neshaneh et ha'olam Ani ve'ata az yavo'u kvar kulam Amru et zeh kodem lefanai Zeh lo meshaneh, Ani ve'ata neshaneh et ha'olam	אֲנִי וְאַתָּה נְשַׁנֶּה אֶת הָעוֹלָם אֲנִי וְאַתָּה אָז יָבוֹאוּ כְּבָר כֻּלָּם אָמְרוּ אֶת זֶה קֹדֶם לְפָנַי זֶה לֹא מְשַׁנֶּה אֲנִי וְאַתָּה נְשַׁנֶּה אֶת הָעוֹלָם אֲנִי וְאַתָּה נְנַסֶּה מֵהַתְחָלָה יִהְיֶה לָנוּ רַע, אֵין דָּבָר זֶה לֹא נוֹרָא אָמְרוּ אֶת זֶה קֹדֶם לְפָנַי זֶה לֹא מְשַׁנֶּה אֲנִי וְאַתָּה נְשַׁנֶּה אֶת הָעוֹלָם אֲנִי וְאַתָּה נְשַׁנֶּה אֶת הָעוֹלָם אֲנִי וְאַתָּה אָז יָבוֹאוּ כְּבָר כֻּלָּם אָמְרוּ אֶת זֶה קֹדֶם לְפָנַי זֶה לֹא מְשַׁנֶּה אֲנִי וְאַתָּה נְשַׁנֶּה אֶת הָעוֹלָם

You & I will change the world

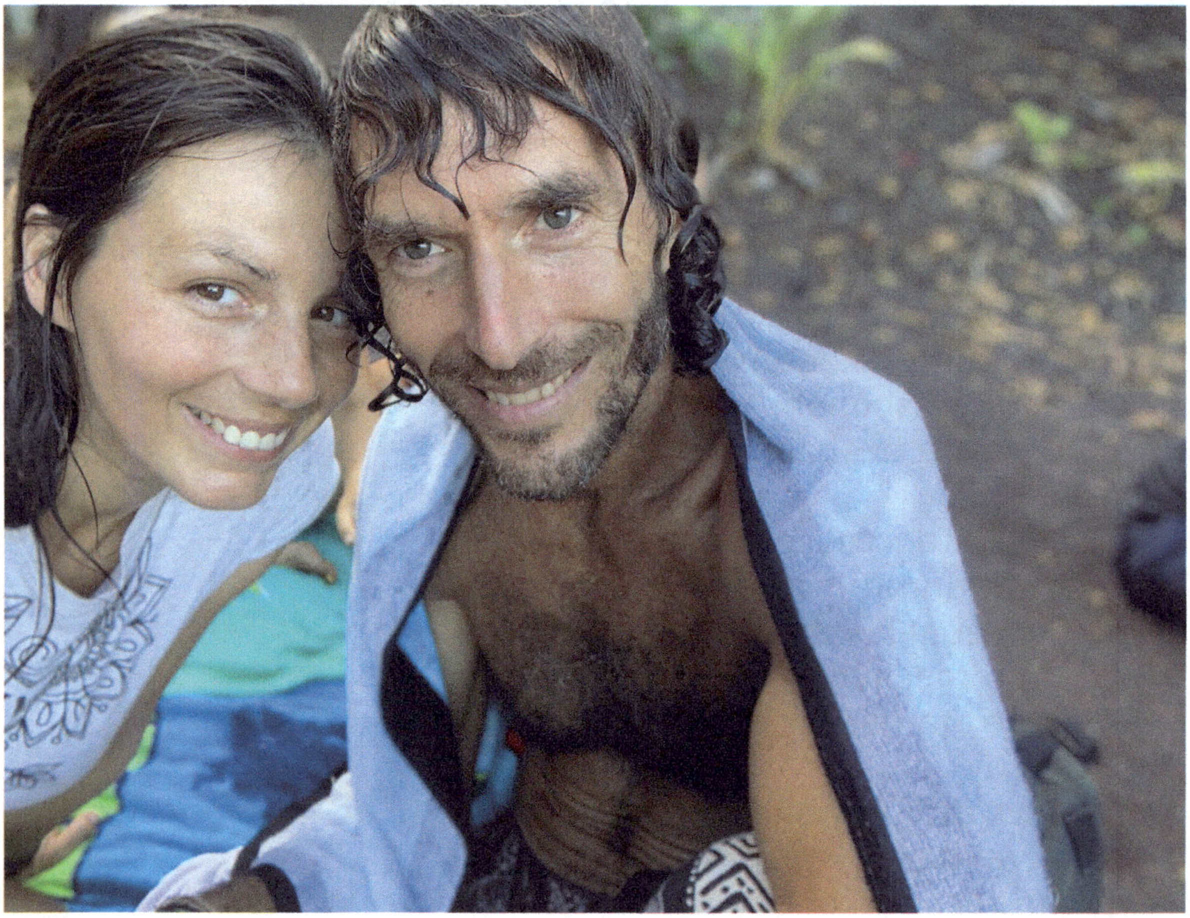

Children's Songs

Every Little Cell

Every little cell in my body is happy
Every little cell in my body is well (2x)

I'm so glad every little cell
In my body is happy and well

A I feel wonderful, I feel wonderful E For this is a glorious day
A I feel wonderful, I feel wonderful
E A And I am going to stay this way
A E A
I'm so glad every little cell in my body is happy and well (repeat)

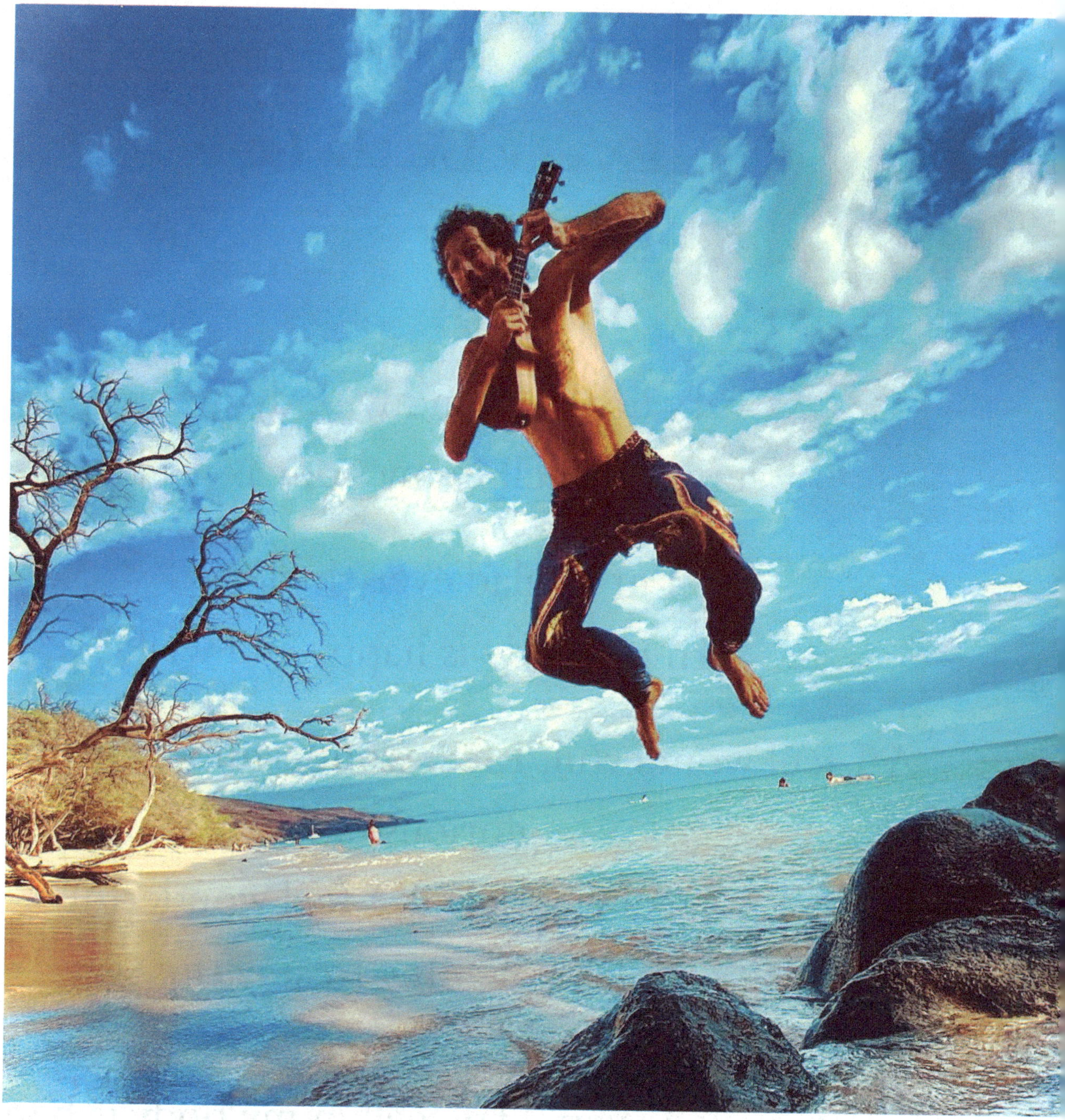

I've Been Working on the Railroad

I've been working on the railroad

All the live long day

I've been working on the railroad

Just to pass the time away

Don't you hear the whistle blowin'

Rise up so early in the morn

Can't you hear the captain shouting

Dinah blow your horn

Dinah won't you blow

Dinah won't you blow

Dinah won't you blow your ho-o-o-orn

Dinah won't you blow

Dinah won't you blow

Dinah won't you blow your horn

Someone's in the kitchen with Dinah

Someone's in the kitchen I know oh-oh-oh

Someone's in the kitchen with Dinah

Strumming on the old banjo

Fee fi fiddle e i o

Fee fi fiddle e i o-o-o-o

Fee fi fiddle e i o

Strumming on the old banjo

Don't you hear the whistle blowin'

Rise up so early in the morn

Can't you hear the captain shouting

Dinah blow your horn

Someone's in the kitchen with Dinah

Someone's in the kitchen I know oh-oh-oh

Someone's in the kitchen with Dinah

Strumming on the old banjo

Fee fi fiddle e i o

Fee fi fiddle e i o-o-o-o

Fee fi fiddle e i o

Strumming on the old banjo

Strumming on the old banjo

Strumming on the old banjo-o-o

Twinkle Twinkle Little Star

(Capo 3) G C G Twinkle twinkle little star
C G D G How I wonder what you are
G C G D Up above the world so high
G C G D Like a diamond in the sky
G C G Twinkle twinkle little star
C G D G How I wonder what you are
G C G Brilla brilla estrellita
C G D G Dime lo que eres tu
C G Luz que brilla en el mar
C G D G Brilla brilla sin parar
C G Brilla brilla estrellita
C G D G Dime lo que eres tu.

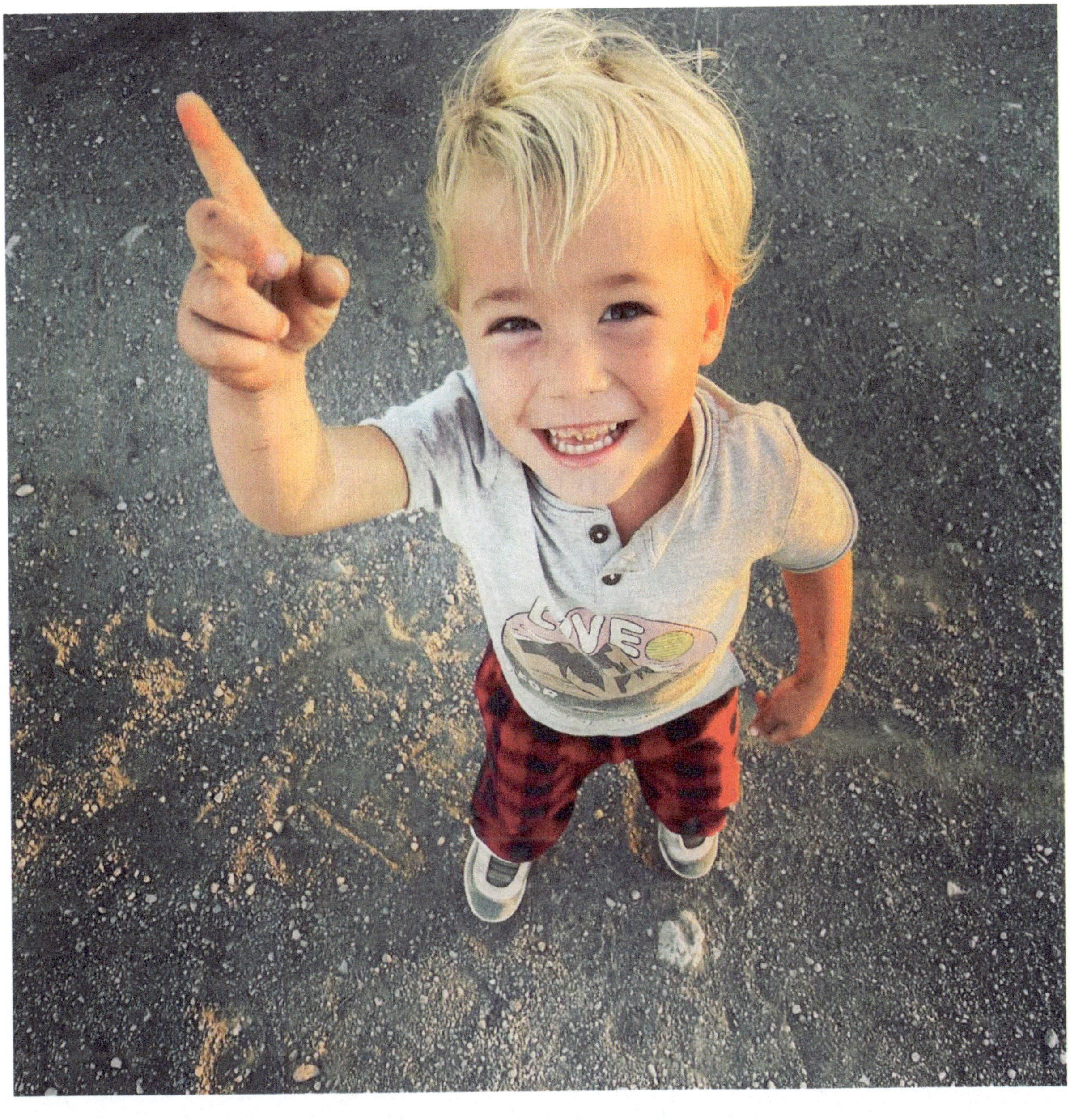

Awaken, Children

Wake up children from your sleeping
Awaken & be glad!
No more crying
No more weeping
No more now be sad!

The morning star is now arising
A new day is at hand
Birds are singing
Bells are ringing
All over the land

Ah!

Awaken, Children, have no worry
of things of future, past
Mother's come
To take us home
& dry our tears at last

Row Row Row Your Boat

Row Row Row Your Boat

Gently Down the Stream

Merrily Merrily Merrily Merrily

Life is But a Dream

Yes! We Have No Bananas
(Frank Silver & Irving Cohn)

C
Bb7 A7
Oh yes, we have no bananas;
   D7   G7
C
We have-a no bananas, to-day.

       F
Fm   C
We've got string beans and onions, and big juicy lemons,
Em
G7
 And all sorts of fruit and say;

    C   F
C
We got an old fashioned to-mah-to,
  F   D7
G7
A Long Island po-tah-to.
   C
Bb7 A7
But yes, we have no bananas;
   D7   G7
C
We have-a no bananas, to-day.

Interlude:

C

C   F   C
G7   C
 There's a fruit store, on our street, who's name is Mr. Peach.
C   F   C
Em   G7
 And he keeps good things to eat; but you should hear him speak!
C   F   C
G7   C
 When you ask him anything; he never answers "no".
G   Gdim
D7   G7
 He just "yes-es" you to death, and then he takes your dough.

C
Bb7 A7
Oh yes, we have no bananas;
   D7   G7
C
We have-a no bananas, to-day.

       F
Fm
We've got a-little beans, and the bigger beans,
       C
And a red beans, and the whiter beans,
Em
G7
 And all kinds of beans and say;

    C   F
C
We got an old fashioned sa-lami;
F
D7   G7
 We even got the Brooklyn pa-strami.
   C
Bb7 A7

Oh yes, we no gotta da banana;
    D7   G7
C
We no gotta da banana to-day.

Solo:

C A7, D7 G7 (x2)

C
C   F   C
G7   C
Business got so good for him, that he wrote home to-day;
C   F   C
Em   G7
"Send me Pete and Nick and Jim; I need help right a-way."

C   F   C
G7   C
When he got them in the store, there was fun, you bet.
G
Gdim   D7
G7
Someone asked for ba-nanas, and then the whole quart-et;
C
Bb7 A7
(Oh yes, we have no bananas),
    D7   G7
C
We have-a no ba-nanas, to-day.

        F
Fm   C

(We've got red beans), (and carrots), (and celery), (and olives),
    Em
G7
But we've got no bananas to-day.

C F C, F D7, G7 (n.C)

C
Bb7 A7
Oh yes, we no gotta da banana;
    D7   G7
C
We no gotta da ba-nana to-day.
Outro:
C D7, C

When We Were Living in Caves

Once upon a time when we were living in caves
We were sittin' 'round the fire and eatin' berry cakes

Then the shaman got up and he began to sing a song
& he said to the people I want you all to sing along

Ha Hoo!

Hoo Ha!

Ha Hoo!

Hoo Ha!

Once upon a time when we were living in caves
We were sitting round the fire and eatin' berry cakes

Then everyone got up and started to dance around
And we all began to make a very crazy sound

Ha Hoo!

Hoo Ha!

Ha Hoo!

Hoo Ha!

Once Upon a Time when we were living in caves
We were sitting round the fire and eatin' berry cakes

Then we all became monkeys and started to really find our bliss
And we all sounded something like this

Ha ha Hoo!!!

Then the shaman lay down and he began to dream

And all the people we did the very same thing

And in the dream we all began to hear a song
And in the dream we all began to sing along...

191

Cottleston Pie

     G F C D
Cottleston Cottleston Cottleston Pie
A fly can't bird, but a bird can fly
Ask me a riddle and I reply
Cottleston Cottleston Cottleston Pie

Cottleston Cottleston Cottleston Pie
A fish can't whistle and neither can I
Ask me a riddle and I reply
Cottleston Cottleston Cottleston Pie

Cottleston Cottleston Cottleston Pie
Why does a chicken? I don't know why
Ask me a riddle and I reply
Cottleston Cottleston Cottleston Pie

Frère Jacques

```
    G D G       G D G
Frère Jacques, Frère Jacques,
   G  C  D     G C D
Dormez-vous? Dormez-vous?
  D7      G      D7      G
Sonnez les matines, sonnez les matines
    C  D  G    C  D  G
Ding dang dong, ding dang dong.
```

(repeat as desired)

English Version:

```
      G D G         G D G
Are you sleeping, are you sleeping?
   G  C  D     G  C  D
Brother John, Brother John?
   D7         G       D7          G
Morning bells are ringing, morning bells are ringing
    C  D  G    C  D  G
Ding ding dong, ding ding dong.
```

Hawaiian Rainbows

Hawaiian rainbows white clouds roll by
I see your colors against the sky
Hawaiian rainbows it seems to me
Come from the mountains down to the sea

Hawaiian rainbows white clouds roll by
I see your colors against the sky
Hawaiian rainbows it seems to me
Come from the mountains down to the sea

Hawaiian rainbows white clouds roll by
I see your colors against the sky
Hawaiian rainbows it seems to me
Come from the mountains down to the sea
Come from the mountains down to the sea

Hawaiian rainbows white clouds roll by
I see your colors against the sky
Hawaiian rainbows it seems to me
Come from the mountains down to the sea

Hawaiian rainbows white clouds roll by
I see your colors against the sky
Hawaiian rainbows it seems to me
Come from the mountains down to the sea
Come from the mountains down to the sea

Ťap, ťap, ťapušky
Pat-a-cake, pat-a-cake
Slovak Clapping Game for Babies

Ťap, ťap, ťapušky,

išli chlapci na hrušky

a dievčatá na jablčka,

postretli tam pána vĺčka

a pán vĺčok hav, hav, hav,

a dievcatka jajajaj.

Pat-a-cake, pat-a-cake,

Boys went to pick up pears

And girls to pick up apples,

They met Mr. Wolf there,

Mr. Wolf said: Woof-woof-woof,

And the girls said: Yow-yow-yow-yow.

Happy Birthday to You
Mildred & Patty Hill

    A   E

Happy Birthday to You...

    E   A

Happy Birthday to You...

    A   D

Happy Birthday Dear [name]...

    D A   E A

Happy Birthday to You...

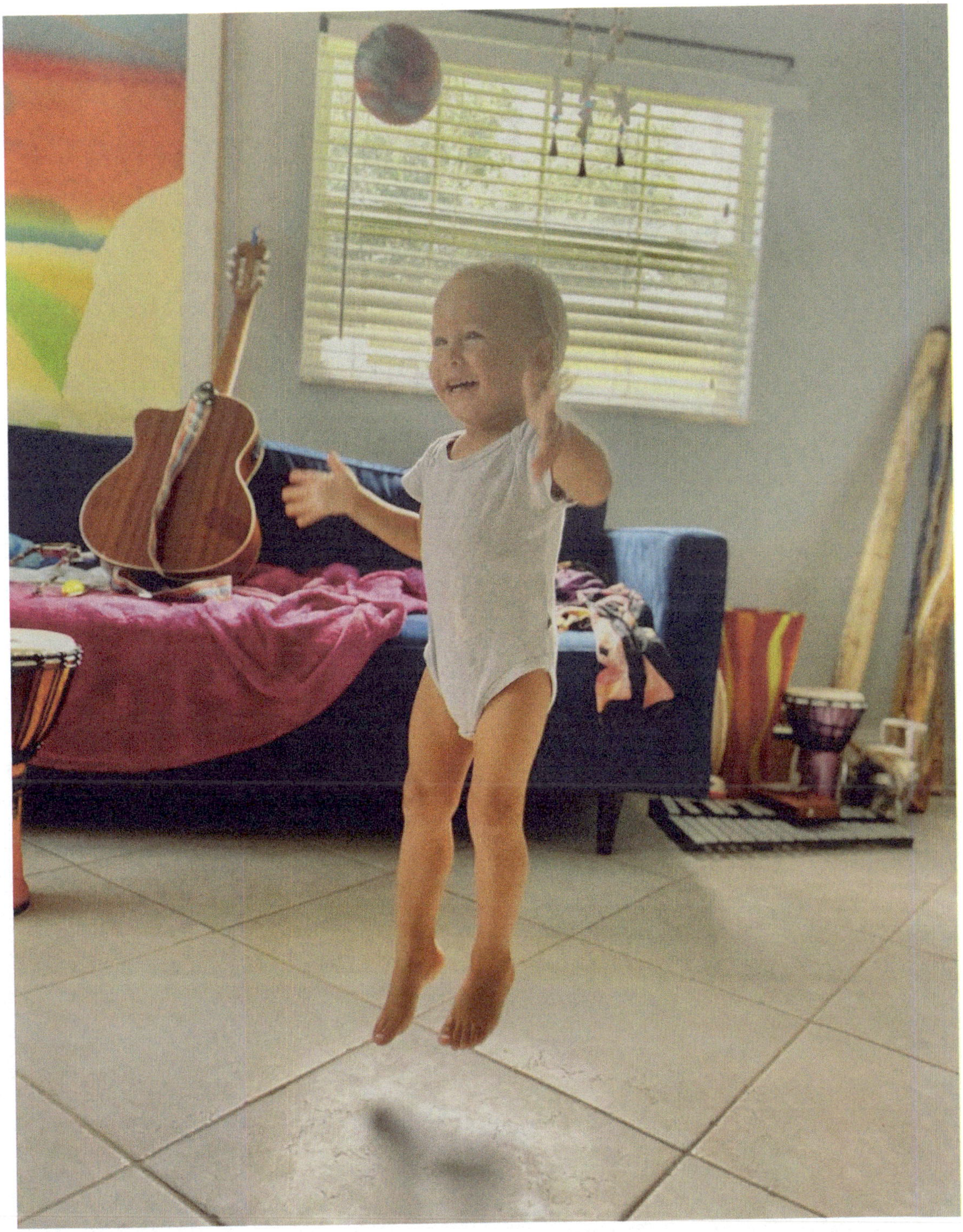

Happy, Happy Birthday!

Alan Sorvall
G C D

Happy Happy Birthday
Happy Birthday to You!

Happy Happy Birthday
Happy Birthday to You!

Na Na Na Na Na Na (repeat)

Happy Happy Birthday...

We Vishnu a Hare Krishna

We Vishnu a Hare Krishna
We Vishnu a Hare Krishna
We Vishnu a Hare Krishna
Rama Hare New Year!

Good Tidings we bring
To you & your kine
Glad Tidings from Krishna
The Cowherd Devine!

Dobrú noc
Good Night
Slovak Lullaby

Dobrú noc má milá,
dobrú noc má milá,
dobrú noc, dobre spi,
nech sa ti snivajù o mne sny.

Good night, my darling,
Good night, my darling,
Good night, sleep well,
I wish I were in your dreams.

LOVE IS THE MUSIC

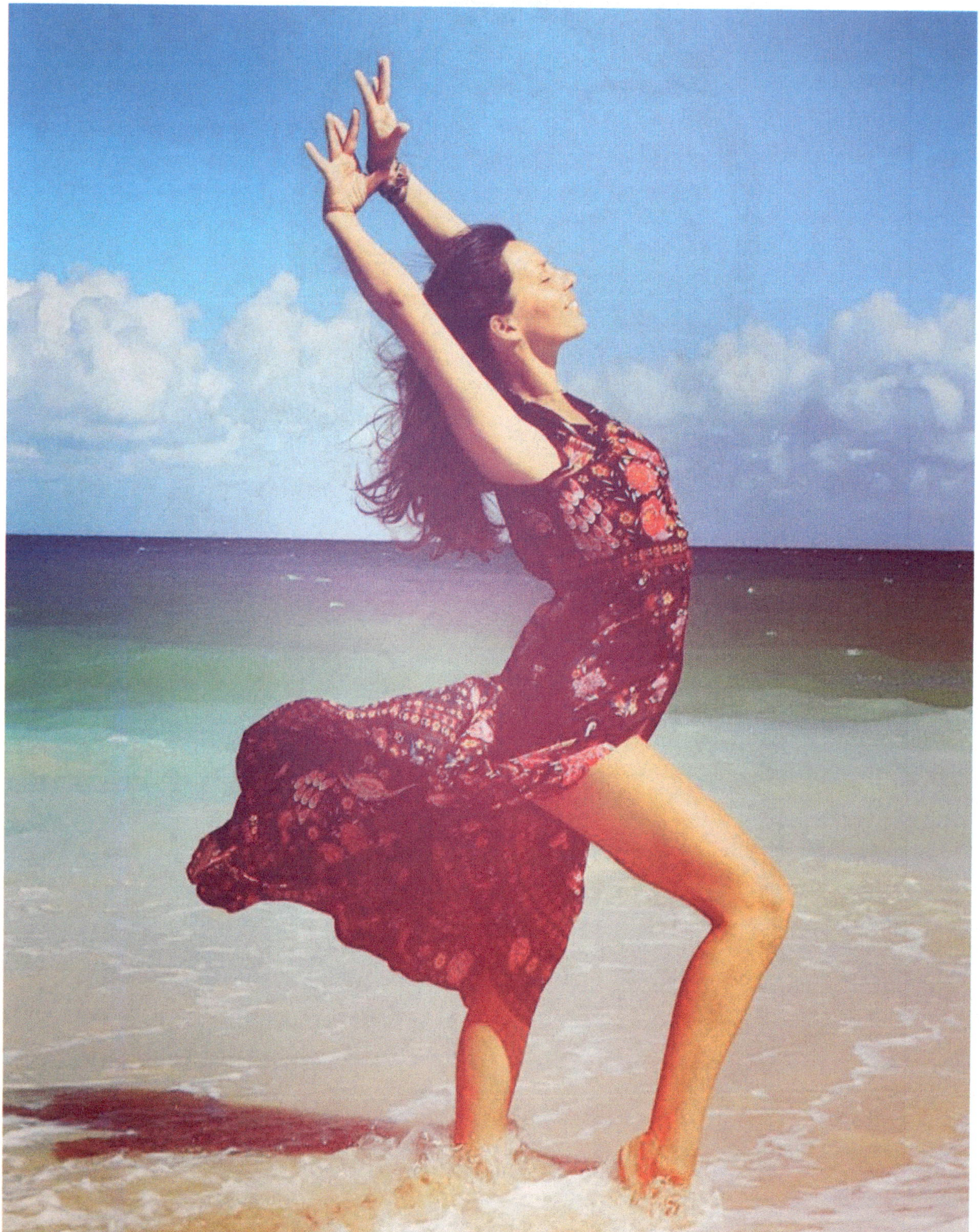

OUR SONGS

Love Is...
The Songbook We Wrote Together

"Well I wonder wonder who – who wrote the Book of Love?"

There is a deeper world than this
& a greater song that we sing
to each other
in eternity
the song of our essential unity
our heartsong
& it is the song we can hear
even now
amidst the cacophony of the world
when, for a moment, we lay aside all differences
& remember our existential undifferentiatedness, our sameness
our nonpreferential *saneness*...
when, rather than reading the black notes on the page.
we read the white spaces in between the notes...
& instead of singing the song of sin once again,
we refrain & choose rather to sing the song of the sun --
the song of the One Son that we all are.
And so, there is no need to ask anyone
"Did you write the Book of Love,
and do you have faith in God above?"
for the answer is YES,
as it's always been & always will.

Love is the Song we wrote together.
Love is the Song we sing together.
Love is the SongBook we are together.

"Love is but a song we sing, fear's the way we die..."

In My Book

♪♪♪

Who wrote the Book of Love?

In my book
you can do no wrong
Just open up & find this song
& when you do, Love
You know it won't be long
That you'll be back where you belong

& though the winds of change
May blow & rage
Still we are gonna be on the
Same page

Taking it slow

Taking our time

Moving forward

To the end of the line...

*In my book
Everyone is alright
Just look within & find delight
We all read the same notes
The same notes day & night
But some read black
And some read white*

*& though the
tone changes
& the notes seem out of tune
Timing's off
the song in ruins
I will be with you girl
Unto the end of the world*

*In my book
you can do no wrong
Just open up & find this song
& when you do, love
You know it won't be long
That you are gonna sing along...*

♪♪♪

Into Her Presence

Capo on 3rd Fret: G to C

Into Her Presence
Will we enter now
Serenely Unaware of Everything
Except Her Shining Face
& Her Perfect Love
Except Her Shining Face
& Her Perfect Love

We have reached the place
where we all are one
And we are home (2x)
Where we are one
& we are home
& we are home

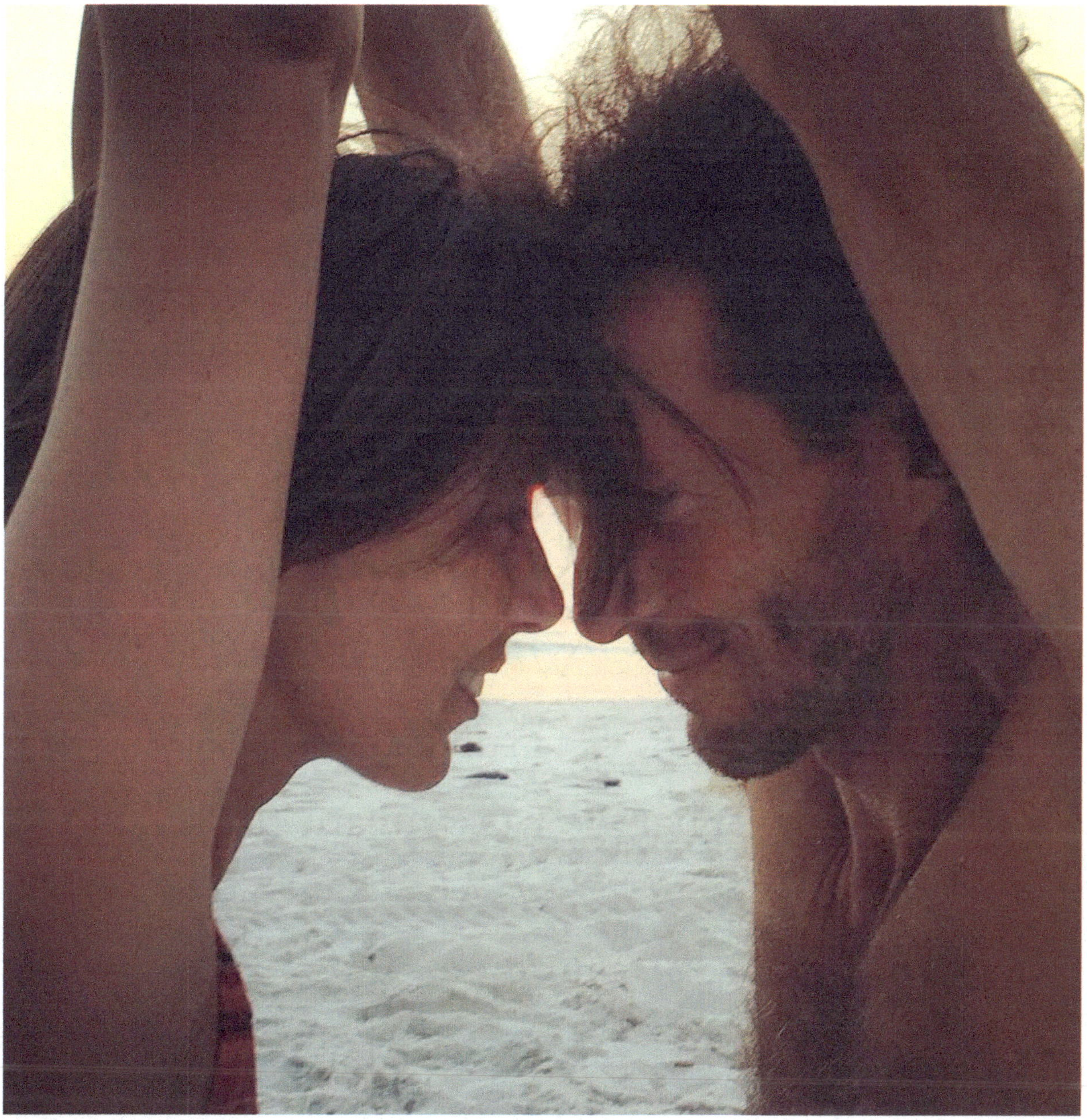

Here We Are

Here we are
We're not far
& here we'll be
Through all the eye can see

You & Me
We will see
Truly see
That we were meant to be
Ah
Here we are
Near not far
& here we'll be
Through all eternity

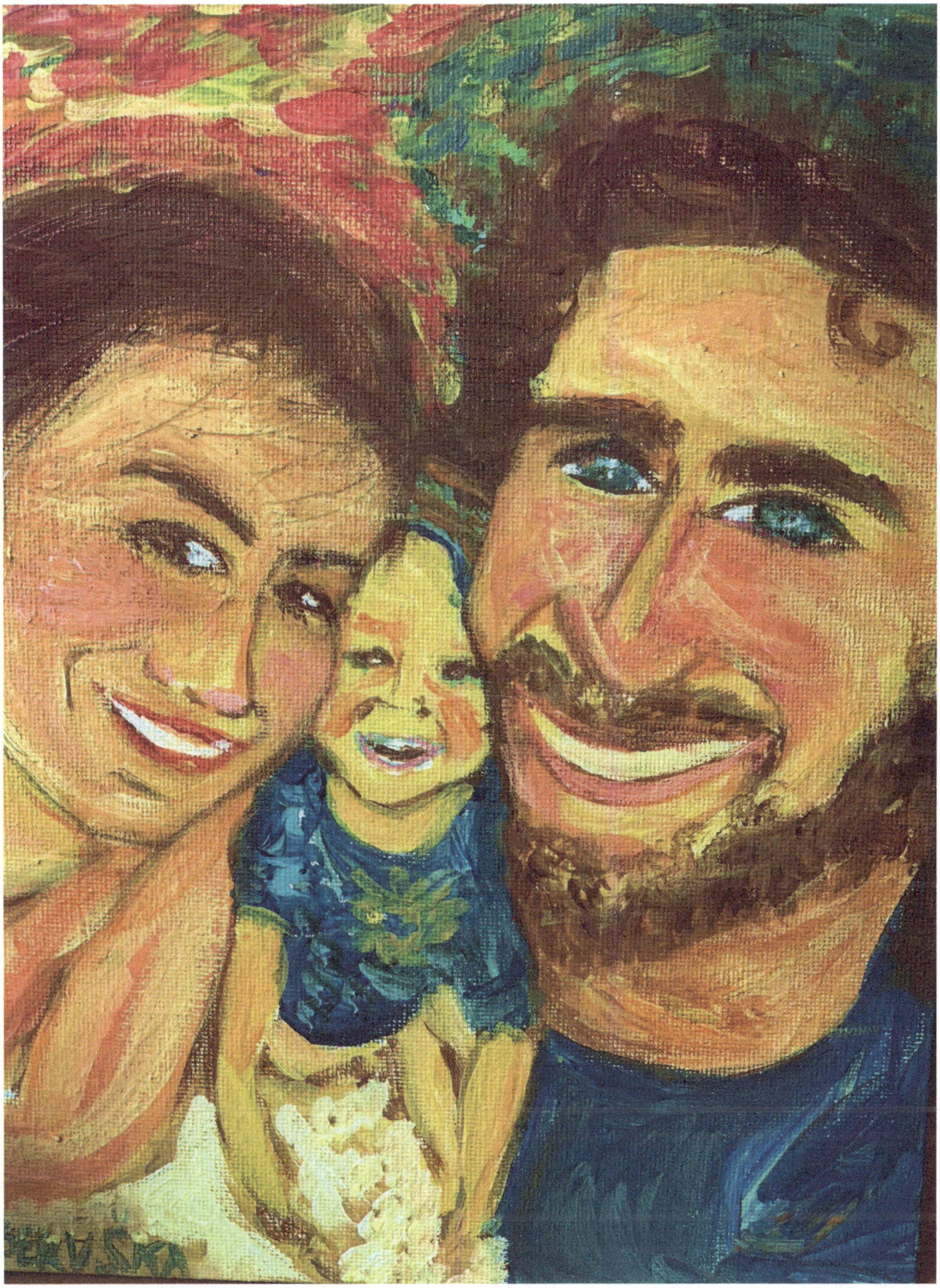

The Forgotten Song

Amaj7 -> A#maj7

"Listen-perhaps you catch a hint of an ancient state not quite forgotten;
dim, perhaps, and yet not altogether unfamiliar,
like a song whose name is long forgotten;
and the circumstances in which you heard completely unremembered.
Not the whole song has stayed with you, but just a little wisp of melody, attached not to a person or a place or anything particular.
But you remember, from just this little part,
how lovely was the song,
how wonderful the setting where you heard it,
and how you loved those who were there and listened with you.

"The notes are nothing.
Yet you have kept them with you, not for themselves,
but as a soft reminder of what would make you weep if you remembered how dear it was to you.
You could remember,
yet you are afraid,

believing you would lose the world you learned since then.
And yet you know that nothing in the world you learned is half so dear as this. Listen,
and see if you remember an ancient song
you knew so long ago and held more dear than any melody you taught yourself to cherish since.

~ A Course in Miracles

The Wings of Song

♪ ♪ ♪

Rise up on the wings of song
Let the sound flow through you
High above the winds of the dawn
As the Spirit moves you
To what you are
To what you are
To who you really are

Break free of these mortal chains & bounds
All the lies that bind you
Free where the voice of love resounds
Let the call remind you
Of all you are
Of all you are
Of all you truly are…

"Know yourself in the One Light
where the miracle that is you
is perfectly clear."

♪ ♪

Rock Steady

♪ ♪ ♪
Are you ready?
Are you ready?
To Rock Steady?
Said are you ready?

We're rockin' thru the night
'til the mornin' light
so get ready

Are you ready?
Are you ready?
To rock 'n' roll?
Get down with soul?

We rockin' all night long
'til the break of dawn
to get ready

Get down to the sound
It's the only dance in town
It's called the Rock Steady
C'mon y'all get ready

We'll show you how to do it
There's really nothin' to it
You just get down in your soul
& you stop.rock.&.roll
♪ ♪ ♪

All Are Called

I enlist you/To be silent/& listen
to your heart

I enlist you/To be silent/& listen
to the calling of your heart

To Be/To Be in Love
To Be/ To Be in Love
To Be (2x)

All are called and few choose to listen
All are called and few choose to listen
All are called, all are called

All are called and few choose to listen (2x)
(do you choose to listen?)
All/You are called, just listen

& Be/ Just Be In Love
& Be/Just Be In Love
& Be (2x)
I enlist you/To be silent/& listen
to your heart (2x)

And Yet Everyone will come Home
Yet Everyone will come Home
Everyone will Listen
And Yes, Everyone will be Free
Yes, Everyone will be Free
Everyone will Be...

Be, Be in Love
Be, Just Be in Love
Be (2x)

I Love You (3x)

Heart & Hands

G C D + Hand Clapping :)

Nothing real can be threatened, Nothing unreal exists
Herein lies the peace of God (3x)

And I place the peace of God in your heart & in your hands
To hold & share (4x)

The heart is pure to hold it & the hands are strong to give it
We cannot lose (3x)
'cause we already won

we already won

we one

we one

& what's the sound of one hand clapping? (2x)
Back to: "Nothing real can be threatened…"

Let's Get Hitched

G Bm7 Am7 C D

Don't die with the music inside you, baby
Don't try to hide it, it'll drive you crazy
Just take my hand
& come and join the band
Hitch your wagon
to a star

You don't have to fight those demons, baby
Don't try to smite 'em, it'll drive you crazy
Just shine a light
It's gonna be all right tonight
Hitch your wagon to a star

Everybody falls for a superstar
Everybody everybody
C'mon now
You know who you are

Don't die with the music inside you, baby
Don't try to fight it, it'll drive you crazy
Just take my hand
I wanna be your man
Hitch your wagon to a star
Hitch your wagon, superstar
Na Na Na

The Music Now

When life feels so unfair
And no one seems to care
Her love flows everywhere
She wants to take you there

Ma

This is your way of being
Just change your way of seeing
Her way is so freeing
My heart is agreeing

Ma

When you learn how to bow
And flow with the Tao
Anyway anyhow
You are the music now

I Am Spirit

As much as you can hear it
& not fear it
I will help you clear it
I Am Spirit
I Am Spirit

I Am Love
Sent here from above
With the message of the Dove
to Love to Love to Love
I Am Love

I Am Peace
Here for your release
Will you accept it, please
for Peace for Peace for Peace
I Am Peace

I Am Joy
Here for every girl and boy
A divine envoy
In joy enjoy in joy
I Am Joy

I Am You
& here's what we must do
To make this dream come true
Come true come true come true
For me & for you

Let's all sing
So to the dawning bring
As we remember everything
Let's all sing
Come sing come sing come sing

We Are Spirit
& Now let's all hear it
We Are Spirit
We Are Spirit
We Are Spirit

I Believe in Miracles

It's never too late to be
The being you always knew you might be
Never too late to see
How great you are
Just come with me

'cause I believe in miracles
I believe in me
I believe in miracles
I believe in you
I believe in me

It's never too late to do
That one damn thing you know you must do
And you know it's up to you
You'll see it through, I believe in you

'cause I believe in miracles
I believe in you
I believe in miracles
I believe in me
I believe in you

You
&
Me
&
Me
&
You
Double U
W-E
WE
'cause you see now
Don't you see
It's not about me
It was never about me
It was all about we
We are the miracle

'cause I believe in miracles
I believe in We
I believe in miracles
I Believe in you
I believe in me

Each of us is a Miracle of Love

The Peace of God is Shining in Me Now

(Open D tuning)

The Peace of God is shining in me now
Let all things shine upon me in that peace
And let me bless them with Peace in me
The Peace of God is shining in me now

I feel the Love of God within me now
Let all things shine upon me in that Love
And let me bless them with the Love in me
The Love of God is shining in me now

225

Love Is Letting Go

Why can't the muse not play forever?
She never stays with me but awhile
& the Universe is a long time waiting
for you to open up & smile
smile

Why can't the flower bloom for all days?
It always slowly fades only to die
And the Heavens are a long time waiting
For you to open up
& cry
Cry

Love is Letting Go (repeat)

Love is letting go of fear
Drawing back this veil of tears
Love is letting go of fear
And love is letting go

Love is letting go of fear
Releasing all these years
this world is not what it appears
Love is letting go

Love is letting go of fear
Releasing all these years
We do not know love here
We do not know

Losin' the Illusion

A D E
♪♪♪

You can fool yourself that this war will make you free
You can fool yourself that the enemy ain't "me"
But true victory is truth
& truth is unity
Gotta learn to teach these eyes to see
The world as one
Where all are brothers
& sisters
All as one

So go on keep lookin' out
For ol' number one
But you know you can only blame yourself
When your hero doesn't come
'cause in this game the winner is the one
Who loses the illusion
Arise great warrior, arise, much work to be done…

To make the world as one
Where all are brothers
And sisters
All as one

Now makin' it all in the family
Makin' the whole wide world my home
And I'm makin' my way
To a brighter day
Tomorrow

The world is one
We all are brothers
& sisters
We are one

Risin' Risin' Above the Battleground…
♪♪♪

Clear As Morning

Your joy is my joy
Your pain is my pain
Your loss is my loss
Your gain is my gain

& I've sung with you
this simple refrain
thru the years & the tears
time & again

It's clear as day
Clear as morning now
Clear the way
No more mourning now
I'm with you
I'm always with you now

I'm with you, though we're still learning how...

And what I really have to say
Can be said any old way...

Open to the day (4x)

Instrumental break

Open to the day
***

Good Cheer

(kapo 3rd fret G D C)

["The Kingdom is perfectly united and perfectly protected, and the ego will not prevail against it. Amen."]

when you feel sad, know this need not be
when you are mad, know this need not be
when you get scared, know this need not be
when you are not wholly joyous, know this need not be

'Cause in this world you need not have tribulation
For I have overcome the world
So be of good cheer
In this world you may have jubilation
Just choose again
& have no fear

Yes be of good cheer
No longer be sad
Yes, have no fear
just rejoice & be glad
rejoice and be glad
rejoice and be glad

yes, have no fear
just rejoice and be glad
just be glad
just be glad

Nothing can prevail against our united will
Nothing can prevail (Every veil must fail)
for we are Love still
United we stand, divided we fall
United we stand, divided we fall

US ANTHEM

Come listen to the song
Out of tune & uptight
Everybody's wrong
But everything is alright

Nothin' good is free
Nothin' good is easy
But take a breath on me
Close your eyes
& maybe baby we will see

see the gleaming through the night
had to lose is all 'fore I saw the light
in the gleaning
what was left was right
& so we do invite
The night

tonight we're gonna lose control
light the fuse & watch her blow
tonight we're gonna get it tight
alright
tonight

tonight we're gonna
fan that spark
every man 'fraid of the dark
tonight we're gonna

Come listen to the song
Out of tune & uptight
Everybody's wrong
But everyone is alright

Nothin' good is free
Nothin' good is easy
But take a breath with me
Close your eyes
& yeah baby we gonna see

see the gleaming through the night
had to lose is all 'fore I saw the light (twilight)
in the gleaning
what was left was right
& so we do invite
tonight

tonight we're gonna lose control
not refuse & watch her blow
tonight we're gonna get it tight
alright tonight

tonight we're gonna
fan that spark
every man 'fraid of the dark
tonight we're gonna
get proof alright
tonight tonight

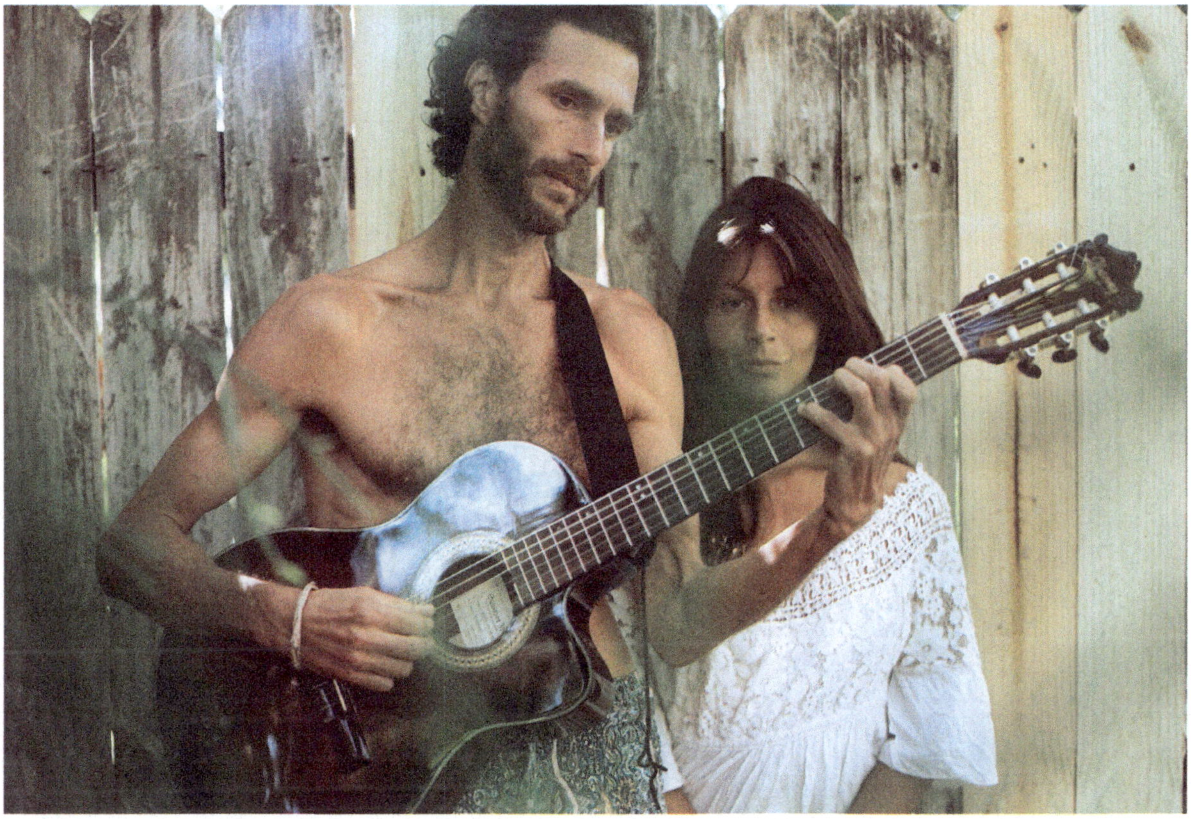

Holy Encounter

When you meet anyone
remember it's a holy encounter
As you see him/you will see yourself

As you treat her/you will treat yourself
As you think of them/you think of yourself
Never Forget this (4x) x2

'Cause in your brother you will find yourSelf
or lose yourself
Yes, in your sister you find yourself or
Lose sight of yourself
And we're really only here to know ourSelf
Yes, we are really only here to know Thyself
& to Thine Own Self Be True
There is nothing else
Nothing else to do/seek here
Nothing else to seek here

*

So when you meet anyone
Remember it's a Holy Encounter
As you see him/you will see yourself
As you treat her/you will treat yourself
As you think of him or her or it
You think of yourself
Never forget this (4x) x4
[On the last time thru,
on the 4th "never forget this," instead sing
"It's a Holy Encounter"]

Are You Coming?

♪♪♪
Baby, this heart is not a plaything
Now please don't try to say anything
Been quiet for too long

Baby, are you coming with me?
You'll have to forgive me
& listen to this song...

Love is not commanding
Never reprimanding
Love is undemanding
Only understanding
Love is patient
Love is kind
I'm gonna give you
a piece of my mind
Take your pick, darlin'
& take your time

Baby, are you goin' my way?
My way is the Highway
It's a longer way to run

Just maybe, you can see it my way?
Maybe give it try anyway
& let's say we lose the gun

Love is not commanding
Never reprimanding
Love is undemanding
Only understanding
Love is patient
Love is kind
Come on baby blow my mind
& maybe somewhere down the line
We gonna find peace of mind, peace of mind,
peace oh mind
♪♪♪

Light of the World
D G A7

I'm still as God created me (3x)
I am the Light of the world

I am the Light of the world
(4x)

I AM the holy Son of God (3x)
I am the Light of the world

I am the Light of the world
(4x)

God is but Love and so am I (3x)
I am the Light of the world

I am the Light of the world
(4X)

I came for the salvation of the world (3x)
I am the Light of the world

I am the Light of the world
(4X)

& Now the Light has come
We are the Light of the world
(4x)

Love Won

♪ ♪ ♪

Out of the darkness,
Into the darkness
One One
is For everyone
but if you want to get to the light
You gotta swim through the night
Fear Nothing,
Love Won

Out of your kindness
Into your blindness
One One
is the only One
& if you want to know the score
you gotta crawl for the sure
Fear Nothing,
Love One

Out of the darkness
Into the darkness
One One
Is forever One
But if you want to get through the night
You gotta call for the light
& it's always darkest before the dawn

Don't Believe the Lie – Love Won

♪ ♪ ♪

My Religion

People ask me all the time
What I believe in
Do I practice some religion
Or what?

My religion is kindness
& I believe in love
There's nothing beside this
& nothing else above

My religion is kindness
& I belongs to the Temple of Love
It's called lovingkindness
& there's nothing else above

OM Mani Padme Hum

Christmas Presence
C F G

The Sun Has Risen
Oh in my Heart
& I shall listen
to what He shall (doth) impart

So pure and innocent
mmm as a little lamb
My Christmas Present
To Know that Love I am (repeat)

Now the Son also rises
In every sing-all Person
& the surprise is
we shine in Unison (repeat)

So Love thy neighbor
Oh 'tis the Season
Become thy savior
In the light of Reason

We'll learn our lessons
Guided by your star
Our Christmas Presence
To Know that Love we are (repeat)

Into Christ's Presence
will we enter now
serenely unaware of everything
except His shining face
and perfect love
*
The Sun Has Risen
Oh in my Heart
Now I shall listen
to what He shall impart

So pure & innocent (you)
As a little lamb
Our Christmas presence
To know that love I am

Be Still
Em A B7

Be Still
& Know
I Am

Be Still
& Know
I Am

Be Still
& Know
I Am

I Am
I Am

Let us be still an instant, and forget all things we ever learned,
all thoughts we had, and every preconception that we hold of what
things mean and what their purpose is.
Let us remember not our own ideas of what the world is for.
We do not know.
Let every image held of everyone be loosened from our minds and
swept away.
Be innocent of judgment, unaware of any thoughts of evil or of good
that ever crossed your mind of anyone.
Now do you know him not.
But you are free to learn of him, and learn of him anew.
Now is he born again to you, and you are born again to him, without
the past that sentenced him to die, and you with him.
Now is he free to live as you are free, because an ancient learning
passed away, and left a place for truth to be reborn.

Be Still
& Know
I Am...

One Life

A -> G
There is one life & that I share with God
There is one life & that I share with God
There is one life & that includes me, too
There is one life
& that I share
with you

I've got one life to live,
one love to give
each day I live
I learn
learn how to give

I've got this one life to live
One love to give
By grace I live
& by grace
I will learn,
learn to forgive

God is just Love
& therefore so am i
God is just Love
& therefore so am I
God is only Love
& that includes you, too
God is only Love
& that I share with you

I've just got this one life
I've just got this one life

God is the Love that is we, too
There is one life & that I share with you

The Attitude of Gratitude

The attitude of gratitude
Is the attitude
That leads to beatitude (2x)

I just want to thank you
I just want to thank you
I just gotta thank you
For being you

I just wanna thank you
I just gotta thank you
Aw thank you, you & all you do
('cause)
The attitude of gratitude
Is that attitude
That grants a little latitude

The attitude of gratitude
Is that Great Attitude
That is the Golden Road to
Blessed Beatitude

& Blessed are the grateful
Blessed are the grateful
'cause even with their plate full
They're not feelin' hateful

Blessed are the grateful
Blessed are the grateful
(dead)
May your plate be full

And may it be full again

& that ain't no platitude, my friend
That's just the platter of food
That's gonna serve you to a better end

I just want to thank you
I just want to thank you
I just need to thank you
You and all you do
I just need to thank you
For being you
(and not being who you are not)

Outro

I just want to thank you
I just need to thank you
And you and you and you and you and you

Attitude of Gratitude

The Risen Sun
(from a poem by Helen Schucman)

Be still, my soul, and rest upon the Lord
In quiet certainty.

For He has come
To rescue you from doubt

And now you stand
In blazing glory of a risen sun
That cannot set.

It will forever be
Exactly as it is.

You stand with Him
Within a radiance prepared for you
Before time was and far beyond its reach.

Be still and know.

And knowing, be you sure
Your Lord has come to you.

There is no doubt
That stands before His countenance,

nor can conceal from you what He would have you see.
The sun has risen.

He has come at last.
Where stands his Presence

there can be no past.

(There can be no past)

Be still, my soul, and rest upon the Lord
Who comes to keep the promise of His Word.

OM NAMO BHAGAVATE VASUDEVAYA

God Is

(Based on A Course in Miracles)

      Bm   A   E
Let me remember what my purpose is
Let me remember my goal is God
Let me remember that there is no sin
Let me remember I am one with God
        G   A
& GOD IS (3x)

Let me forget my brother's past today
Let me perceive no differences today
Let me not bind your Son with laws I made
Let all things be exactly as they are
GOD IS   (3x)

Let me see the ego's twisted game
Let me see that it is insane
And let me see beyond this world where illusion reigns
Beyond Time & Space, Sadness & Pain
GOD IS

Live On Love

G C D Aminor

I live on love
I live on love
I live on your sweet love
& I don't need nothin' else to hold me
little birdie told me
not to worry anymore...

'cause nothin' is ever wrong
I'm always where I belong

nothin' to be scared of
everything is taken care of

I live on faith
I'm a'livin' on faith
I'm livin' on faith alone
& I'm always goin' home
know I'm gonna get there
& mama I don't care
just how long it's gonna take

ain't wastin' time no more
now I know there ain't no time to waste!

Can't make no mistake
Living in a state of perfect grace

I live on love, I live on love...

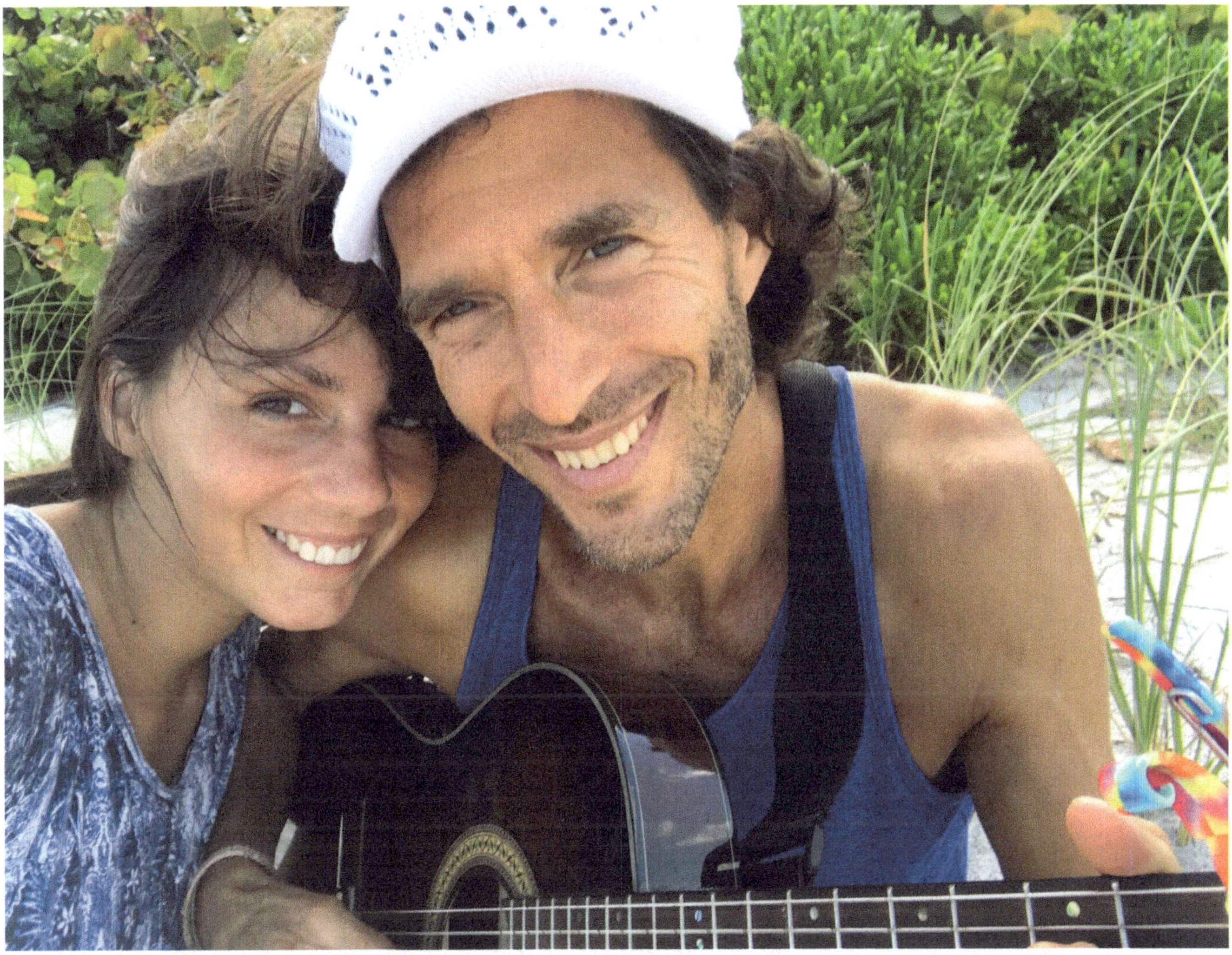

Walk In Glory

G D C D

If you knew who walked beside you
on the way that you have chosen
fear would be impossible

If you but knew the meaning of His Love,
fear would be impossible

So walk you in glory with your head held high
And fear no evil for I walk there by your side (2x)

*

Look up and see his word among the stars
Where God set your name along with His

Look up and see your certain destiny
That the world would hide but He would have you see

So walk you in glory with your head held high
And fear no evil for I walk there by your side (2x)
By your side
*
"Be not afraid.
We only start again an ancient journey long ago begun that but seems new.
We have begun again upon a road we travelled on before
and lost our way a little while.
And now we try again."

SHALOM   SHANTI OM

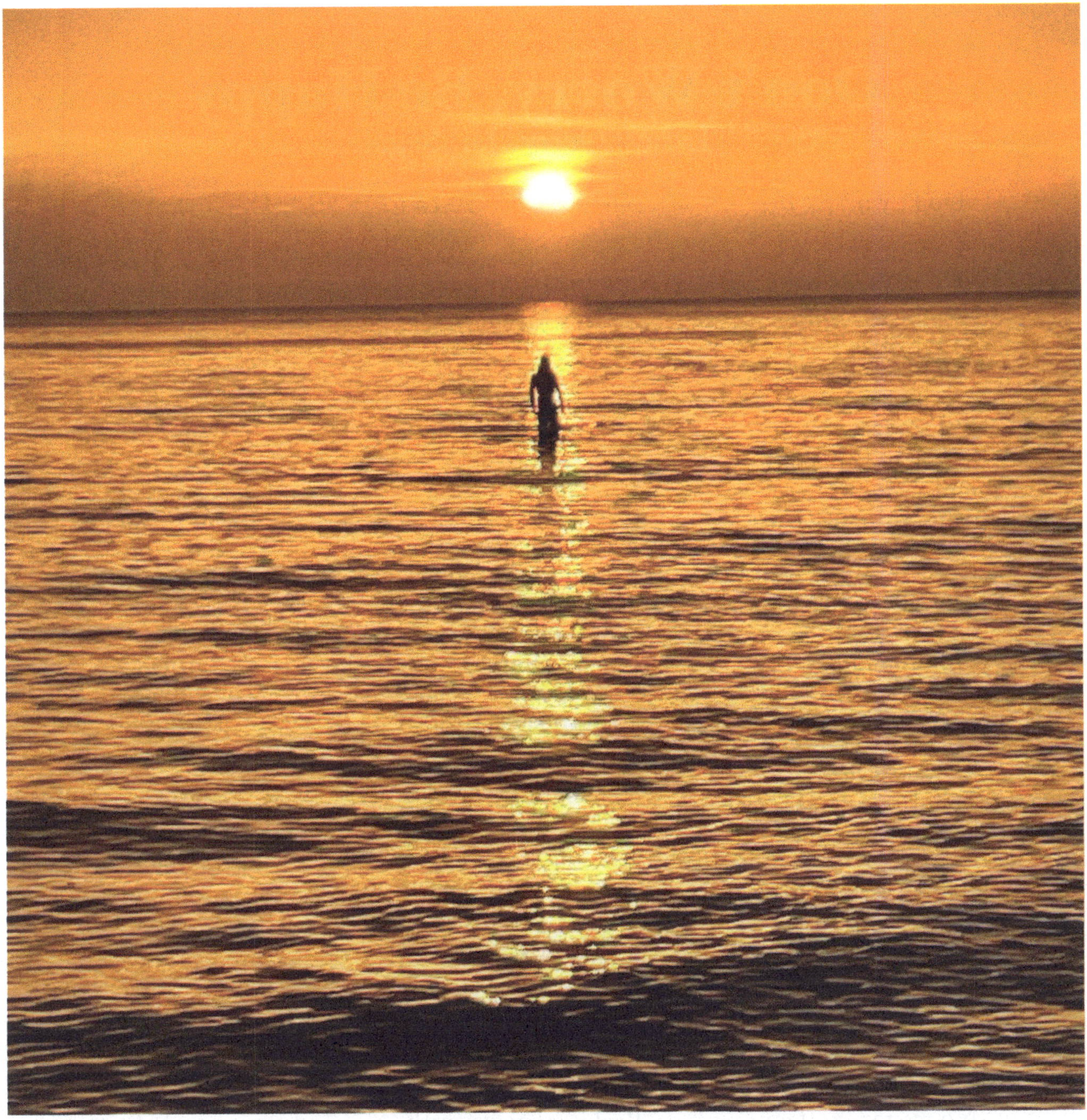

Don't Worry, Be Happy
Lyrics: Gerry "Jai" Segal

Don't worry, Be happy
Life is good, Getting better
My heart, is open
Only love inside
Only love inside

I have, all I want
I need, nothing more
I embrace, my destiny
With faith and trust

Knowing all, is well
My dreams, all come true
From happiness, to joy-From joy, to bliss
My cup is full
Thank you God for this gift
Thank you God for this gift

Don't worry, Be happy
Life is good, Getting better
My heart, is open
Only love inside
Only love inside

No worry, No fear
No anger, No hate
Getting stronger, Getting wiser
I pursue my dreams

I know, what's real
Life is, a dream
Now here, soon gone
What is my legacy?

Don't worry, Be happy

Life is good, Getting better
My heart, is open
Only love inside
Only love inside

Open eyes, look around
Beauty, everywhere
I am, so lucky
To have this life

I've received, so much
How do I, give back?
I will teach, I will mentor-I will set an example
My purpose is to serve
My purpose is to serve

Don't worry, Be happy
Life is good, Getting better
My heart, is open
Only love inside
Only love inside

Close eyes, feel the love
A round me, all the time
Bask in, the warmth
Everywhere is my home

All things, are good
There are, no mistakes
Do not, seek comfort
Embrace, adversity-Which makes me strong
After rain comes sun
No reason to complain

Don't worry, Be happy
Life is good, Getting better
My heart, is open
Only love inside
Only love inside

I heal, my wounds
Let go, of the past
I did, the best I could
Now it's time, to move on
Forgive myself, and others
Forgive myself, and all others
Face my, dark shadows
Then they, melt away

I am, child of God
Help me, to remember
Sacred life, so profound
Thank you for this lesson
Thank you for this lesson

Don't worry, Be happy
Life is good, Getting better
My heart, is open wide
Only love inside
Only love inside
(repeat paragraph)

Only love is real

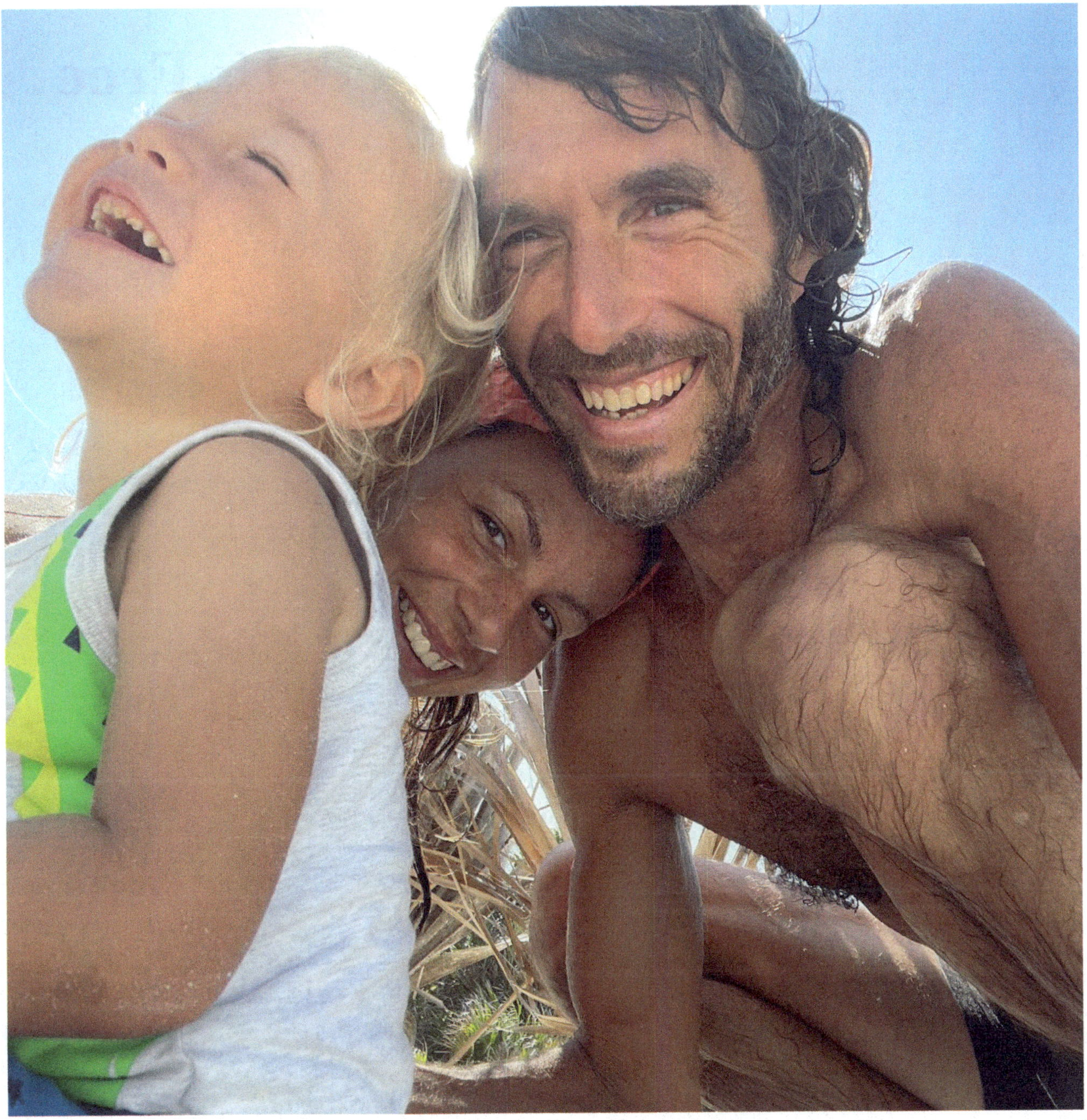

Forgiveness Sets Us Free

♪♪♪
Some say Love makes the world go 'round
Love
makes the world go 'round
Love
Love...

& I say
Yes, I say

Fear binds the world,
Forgiveness sets it free

Fear binds the world,
Forgiveness sets you free

& I love you
more than the stars above you
more than words tell of you
more than I can say

& I say
Yes, I say

Fear binds the world,
Forgiveness sets it free

Fear binds the world,
Forgiveness sets you free...

♪♪♪

"You who want peace can find it only by complete forgiveness."

~ A Course in Miracles

Holy Mother Full of Grace

Holy Mother full of grace
I will ever seek thy face
Let me never fall from grace
Let me never leave this place

MA
JAI MA

Holy Mother full of grace
Savior of the human race
Hold me in thy kind embrace
& let me never fall from grace

Holy Mother full of grace
      Will you ever show your face?
I'll ever be a fool for grace
For I would ever know thy ways

Holy Mother full of grace
Hold me in thy kind embrace
& LET ME NOW YOUR VEIL UNLACE
FOR I WOULD EVER KISS THY FACE
FOR I WOULD EVER KISS THY FACE

MA
JAI MA

I could never fall from grace
I could never leave this place
For I am ever full from grace
And here I'll ever stay
'til the end of my days

Fight In the Dog

They said it was impossible
They said that it couldn't be done

They panned it and they banned it
Before you had even begun

Thank God you didn't listen
Thank God you fought your way thru the fog

you unleashed the fury
unleashed the
fight in the dog

Free Yourself
Be Yourself
Be Yourself
Free Yourself

They said you'd never make it
That never the twain shall meet
But you kept comin'
You kept drummin'
'Cause you knew you had the system beat

You put the fudge in the formula
Said I ain't gonna be no cog
It's not the size of the log in the fire
It's the fight in the dog

Free Yourself
Be Yourself
Be Yourself
Free Yourself

They said there is no way
You said there is no they...

'Til The Break of Day
♪♪♪
I am in love
I'm so in love
Heaven above
My love, my dove, my love…

& here I'll stay
With you my lay-day
All night and day
Until the break of day

And here I'll stay
With you my lady
All night and day
Oh hark! the break of day…
♪♪♪

Return to the Garden of Love

E F#m G#m F#m E

Things have changed
as they will

& still my heart, my love, returns there still
To those days of bliss,
It was enough
When we dwelt content in the Garden of Love

Ah but things were purer, simpler there
My heart had ne'er a pimple, ne're a care
Beyond this world of flurry, fluff & stuff
Return with me, my Love, to the Garden of Love

Why did we ever have to leave?
That it was an error, I never will believe
We returned but to bear the message of the dove
That all will presently dwell in the Garden of Love

Return
Return
Return
Return
To the Garden of Love
To the Garden of Love
To the Garden of Love

I Will Be Still A Moment

(Kapo on 3rd fret, G & C for most)

I will be still a moment and go home
I will let the music take me back to true love
& listen for that forgotten song that I once knew
I will be still a moment and go home (2x)

I am in need of nothing but the truth
That love which created me is what I am
& let every voice but God's be still in me
& let the truth set me free
Let me still & listen to the truth (2x)

I am
I am already home
The Light Has Come

Let's be still a moment & go home

The hush of heaven holds our hearts to hear
A still, small voice & forgotten song
That we once knew
Let's be still a moment & go home
Let's be still a moment & go home
Go Home
Go Home
Let me be still
I will be still

Everyone Knows What Love Is

(everyone knows what)

Love is

(& yet it seems, nobody knows just what)

Love is

(do you know what?)

Love is

(& it isn't what you think)

Love is

('cause just when you think you know what)

Love is

(it is almost certainly *not* what)

Love is

(for in human terms we know not what)

Love is

(while in our Divine Reality we rest in **That**)

Love Is

Truly Helpful

C G & F

I am here only to be truly helpful.

I am here to represent the One who sent me.

I do not have to worry about what to say or what to do, because the One who sent me will direct me.

I am content to be wherever Spirit needs me to be, knowing Spirit goes there with me.

I will be healed as I let Spirit teach me to heal.

~ **A Course in Miracles**

So Long

Baby you rock me to the coeur
And now you've got me down on the floor
You are the one I've been waiting for
For so long

For so long now I've been on the road
Hiding out in the cold
A lonely traveler gone solo
For so long

For So long, I've been gone
For so long, we'll be rocking on
For so long

Rock On
Roll On

You Are the One I've Been Waiting For

Baby we can now end this detour
And you&I will go on tour
We are the One we've been waiting for
For so long

We Are the One We've Been Waiting For

For so long
We've been gone
For so long, we'll keep rocking on
For So long

You are the One I've been/I am the One you've been
You are the One you've been/We are the One we've been...
waiting for, for so long...

Bless You, Brother

C to Dminor

I bless you brother with the Love of God
Which I would share with you for I would learn
The joyous lesson that there is no Love
But God's and yours and mine and everyone's

(Aminor Eminor D G)

There is no Love but God's
And we are all there
There is no Love but God's
And it is for us to share
Here There & Everywhere
It is.....
for us to share

I Bless You Brother...

Love Is Here
F C Dminor Bflat

Have no fear
Of shadows near
Just remember dear
That Love is here

Love is...hear
so very near
now lay aside all fear
and be still my dear

Be still my dear
Love is always here
The way is clear
Beyond all fear

Beyond all fear
Beyond all fear
Beyond all fear
Love is here

Have no fear
Of shadows near
Just remember dear
That Love is here

Love is...hear
so very near
now lay aside all fear
and be still my dear

Be still my dear
Love is always here
The way is clear
Beyond all fear

Beyond all fear
Beyond all fear
Beyond all fear
Love is here

State of Grace

D G A

Spirit is in a state of grace forever
Our reality is only spirit
We are in a state of grace forever 2x

step into that everflowin' river
out beyond the shores of tide & time
& so forgiveness comes to the forgiver
& so we surely claim what's yours & mine
yours&mine

& I have loved you for forever
never was a time when we've been apart
and all we need do is to remember
the truth buried deep within the heart

remember

Forever&ever&ever&ever&ever
Endeavor – until the end of endeavors
remember

Step into that Everflowin' river
Cast your sin upon the sunlight there
& So Forgiveness comes to the Forgiver
& So we sing again a song of prayer

Ready for Love

Are you open to hearing your heart's song?
Are you willing to put nothing else above?
Are you ready to stop thinking your part's wrong?
Are you ready, ready for love

Are you ready to let go of all your worry?
Are you ready to release all fear?
Are you ready to see no sense in hurry?
Are you ready to see it's already here?

Are you ready to accept t/his invitation?
Are you ready to release control?
Are you ready to see no separation?
Are you ready to see your brother whole?
Ready for love?

Ready for Love?
Are you ready for Love?

And these words whisper in the wind and the sunshine
And this song sings softly in your heart
And this all has been already deep on your troubled mind
And this question is secretly tearing...tearing you apart
Are you ready for Love?

Just let go, and you will know
There was nothing to let go of

Just let you be & you will see
There was only
ever love

I am here only to be truly helpful.

I am here to represent Him Who sent me.

I do not have to worry about what to say or what to do,
because He Who sent me will direct me.

I am content to be wherever He wishes,
knowing He goes there with me.

I will be healed as I let him teach me to heal.

A Course in Miracles

How Lovely

How lovely is the world whose purpose is forgiveness of God's Son!
How free from fear, how filled with blessing and with happiness!
And what a joyous thing it is to dwell a little while in such a happy place!
How free from fear, how filled with blessing and with happiness!
Nor can it be forgot, in such a world,
it is a little while till timelessness comes quietly
to take the place of time.

Swear not to die, you holy Son of God!
You make a bargain that you cannot keep.
The Son of Life cannot be killed.
He is immortal as his Father.
What he is cannot be changed.
He is the only thing in all the universe that must be one.
What seems eternal all will have an end.
The stars will disappear, and night and day will be no more.
All things that come and go, the tides, the seasons and the lives of men; all things that change with time and bloom and fade will not return. Where time has set an end is not where the eternal is, the eternal is... Love Is.

Happy Unbirthday to Me

If I was all the way there, well I wouldn't be here
I wouldn't have a care, I would have no fear
Fall back into Love & just completely disappear
If I was all the way there, I wouldn't be here

Yeah if I was all right, there'd be nothing left
Life would no longer be such a matter of life and death
The wonder of it all would finally take away my breath
And it would all be alright, because there'd be nothing left

So Happy Unbirthday to Me
Yeah I think I'm finally, finally starting to see
That it's not all about me -- it's all about we
Happy Unbirthday birthday to Me
(but wait, there's more...)

If I was all here, I'd already be there
my melodramatic old friend the ego just wouldn't have a prayer
But you know to be now and here is to be nowhere
And now I'm not all here
So I guess I'm not all there

So I'll just keep singing this little unbirthday song
And invite y'all to come on and sing along
& consider if it ain't all right, then it might just be all wrong
& yet it won't be long, no it won't be long...
'Til we're all all here and we're all all there
& in fact we are all all right everywhere
& nowhere do you end and me declare
that this is all neither here nor there
so happy unbirthday to me...

For the Love of God
E A B F#minor

For the Love of God please come home!
Ohhh for it be thy will

For the Love of God please be kind to yourself
'cause if you don't, nobody else will

Please Come Home (3x)
Right now

For the Love of God
Please come clear
And you know you will

For the Love of God
You're doing this all to yourself
This is your will

Please Come Home (3x)

'cause if not now, then when?
'cause if not now, it will surely be then

Oh Oh Oh (3x)

'Cause if it's not one thing, it's another
Don't you see it's all the same, all the same
One way or the other?

Oh Damn your confusion
Gotta see clear thru this illusion
Right now

Right
Right
Right
Now
For the Love   For the Love   For the Love

"Without your smile the world could not be saved."

(By Beruschka)

Song of a Sunflower

♪ ♪ ♪

D G A
Open up, morning sun
Open up, precious one
Come on now
I'm so lonely
Come on out
& play with me

Your Smile, Your Smile is everything...

Open up, darling one
Open up to the sun
Open now to the day
Come on now
We two shall play

C'mon!

♪ ♪ ♪

Stay Wild

Sunny Day
Funny Way
That you've got
To make me say
Ahhhhh

Don't let this world ever tame you
Don't let their words ever shame you
Don't let anyone ever blame you
Don't take the blame

Stay wild my child
Running free
To Be the beauty
You were born to be
Born to Be

And may you know
Wherever you go
Through the wind & snow
Wherever you go

We love everything that you are
We love everything that you are
You are our star
You are perfect to me

Stay wild my child
Running free
To be whatever
You're meant to be

Sunny Day
Funny Way
That you've got
To make me stay
Ahhhhh

Let It Be Undone

D -> A
♪ ♪ ♪
Now we are together
These birds of a feather
Flying Together
In all kinds of weather
Flying Forever
Now & Forever

& all we need to do, all we need do
Is to gather together
Never mind the weather

'Cause Now it's forever
Now it's forever

& It's already done
In the name of The One
Flying to the Sun

So let it be undone
Yes, it can be undone
In the name of The One
it is already undone
all ready done
All Ready?...One
♪ ♪ ♪

Sunsmile

D G & A

Oh how I love just to see you smilin'!
Clouds up above is where the sun's been hidin'...
Clouds Clouds Roll Away
Sun Come on Out Today
Little Children Wait to Play
Won't You Smile Upon this cold, gray lonesome day?

Do you remember when we were young at heart,
Faces lit up so bright so radiant?
Sure the rain did fall & tears we cried
But there was warmth and joy inside
Now there ain't no reason more to hide
You were a friend in whom I could rely on, child
& oh How I love just to see you smilin'
Oh how I love just to see you smile!

Bridge
Child awaken
Day is breakin'
Rise & Shine
Those streamin' eyes

'Cause you know I don't like to see you cry
hate to see any sadness in your eyes
I would give anything to make it alright

So cheer up now
Let's enjoy this day
It's clearin' up out
Sunshine is on the way
We are all waiting here just to see you smile...
SMILE
SMILE
SMILE repeat
Oh How I Love to See You Smilin' (repeat over & over)

Come Home

"Listen to the story of the prodigal son, and learn what God's treasure is and YOURS: This son of a loving father left his home and thought he squandered everything for nothing of any value, although he did not know its worthlessness at the time. He was ashamed to return to his father, because he thought he had hurt him. Yet when he came home, the father welcomed him with joy because only the son himself WAS his father's treasure. He WANTED nothing else."

Forever Have I Loved You

Forever Have I Longed for You

Forever Have I Missed You

Forever Have I Called to You

Forever

Forever

COME HOME

"There is no death because the Son of God is like his Father. Nothing you can do can change Eternal Love. Forget your dreams of sin and guilt, and come with me instead to share the resurrection of God's Son. And bring with you all those whom He has sent to you to care for as I care for you."

May I have this
One Dance
Sun Dance
The boundlessly bountiful bounty
Of AbunDance...?

One Dance

♪ ♪ ♪

Come Dance
One Dance
The Boundlessly Bountiful Bounty
Of Abundance

Come Dance
Sun Dance
& Have a Good One

When I look at the morning sun
I feel life has just begun
When I look at you & me
I feel happy, I feel free

Come Dance
One Dance
The Resolutely Irresistible Rhythm
Of Non-Resist-Dance

Come Dance
It's a fun dance
& Have a Good One

When I look at the morning sun
I feel life has just begun
When I look at you & me
I feel happy, I feel free...

♪ ♪ ♪

"*Your Love is like a rainbow…*"

To Change the World

A D E
♪♪♪
You can't change the world
You can only change your mind
You can't change it, girl
You can only learn to be more kind

& when we do
I'm tellin' you
Together we may find…

That we CAN change the world
When we change our mind

And the Band Played On
& On & On & On & On…

(You can't change the moon,
You can only change your tune!)

♪♪♪

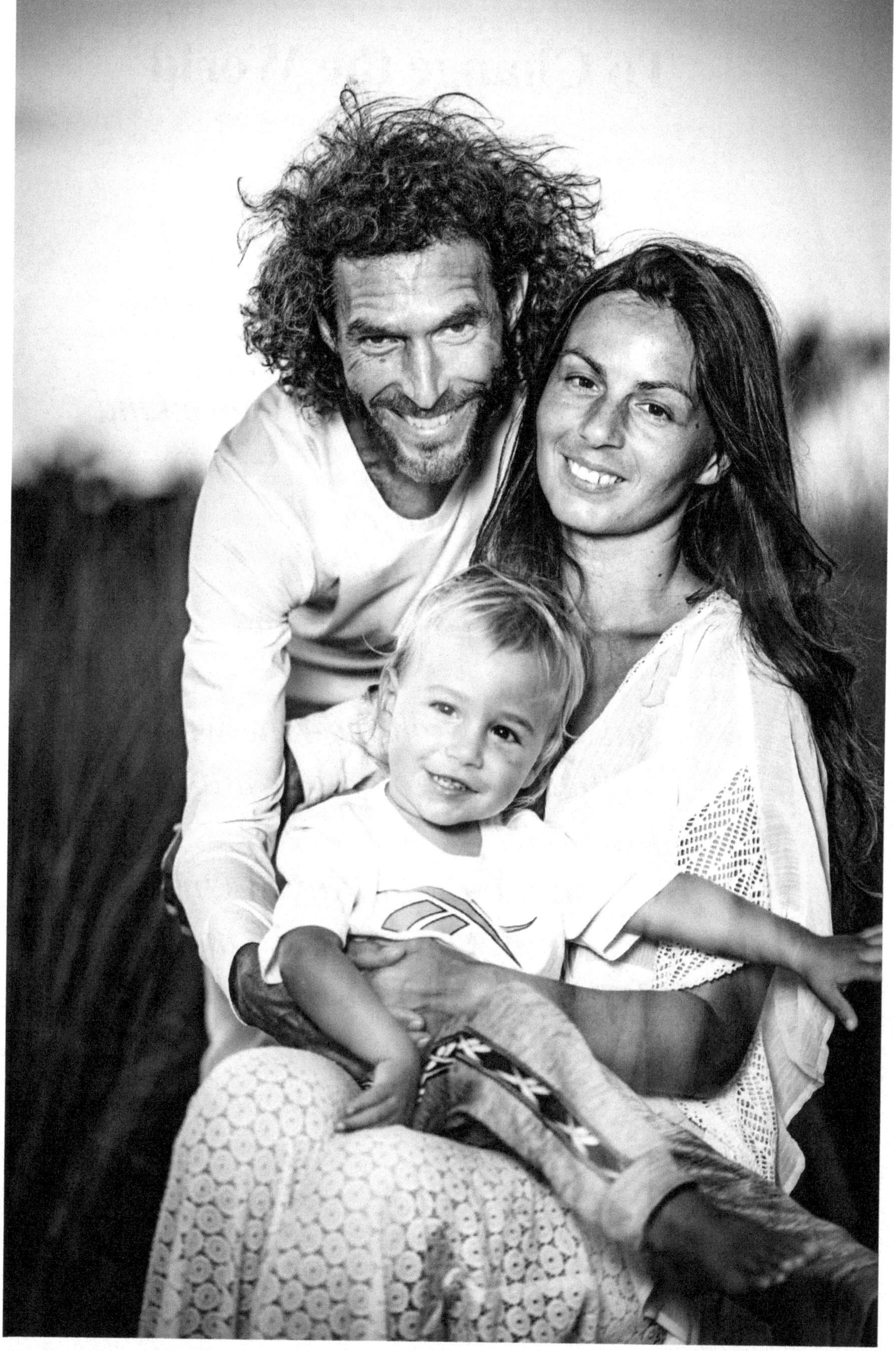

JAH MAKEAH, NO PROBLEM

♪ ♪ ♪
Jah!
Jamaica no problem

Jah!
Jah Makea no problem

I am
Still as Jah created me

I am
Still as Jah Jah created me

In the light, in the love
In the glory

Gotta to get our jam on
Gotta get y/our jah mon

Jah!
Jamaica no problem
So why ya makin' a problem?

Jamaica no problem
So what seems to be the problem, mon?
♪ ♪ ♪

"Listen my friends... so outta sight, bein' in love!"

Beata took this pic of me on the day we first met, Dec 25th, 2017.

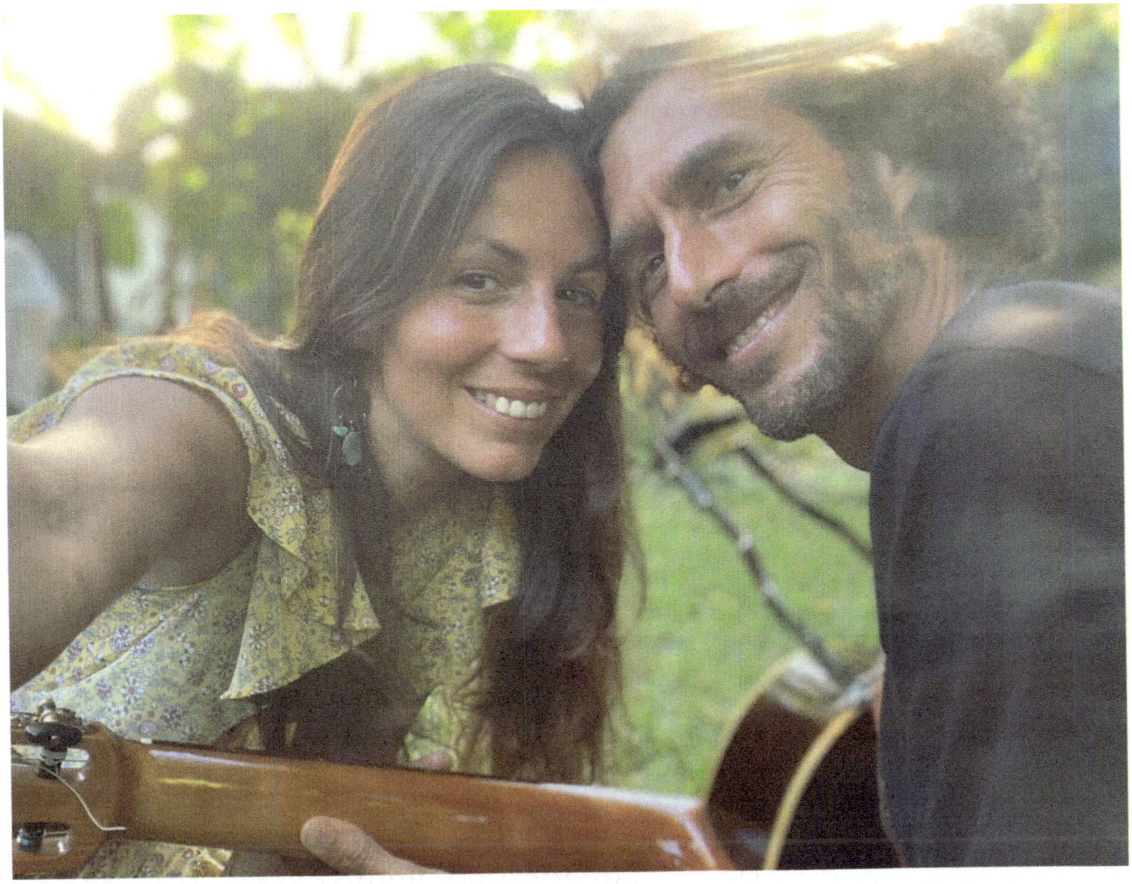

CHOOSE ONCE AGAIN

♪ ♪ ♪

I am still as Love created me

I am still as Love created me

I am still as God created me

I am still as God

I am still as God created me

His Son can suffer nothing

& I am His Son, I am His Son

In every difficulty

In all distress, in each perplexity

Christ calls to you & gently says,

"*My brother, choose again.*"

We are still as Love created We

We are still as God created We

We are still as Love created We

We are still as God

♪ ♪ ♪

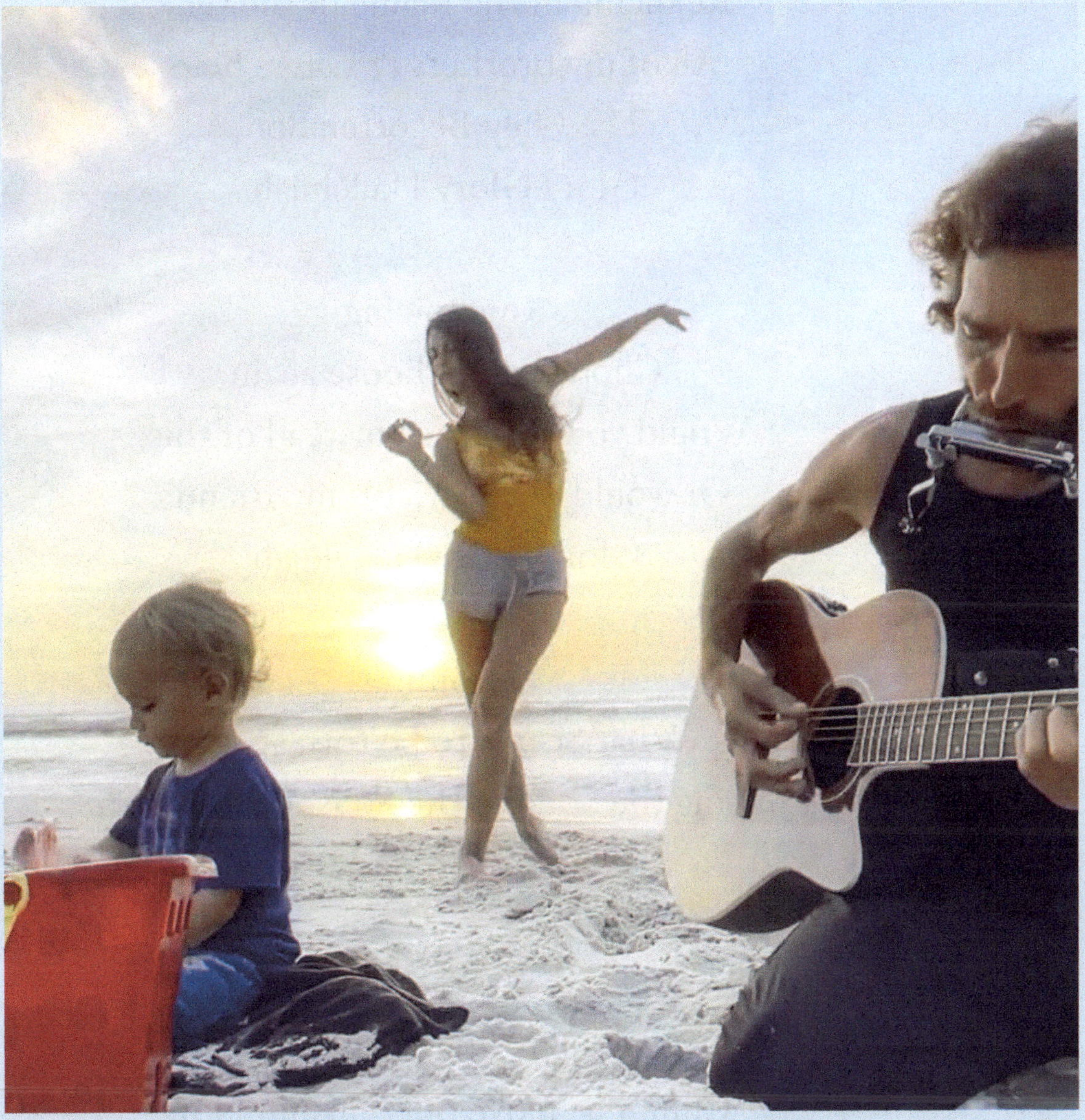

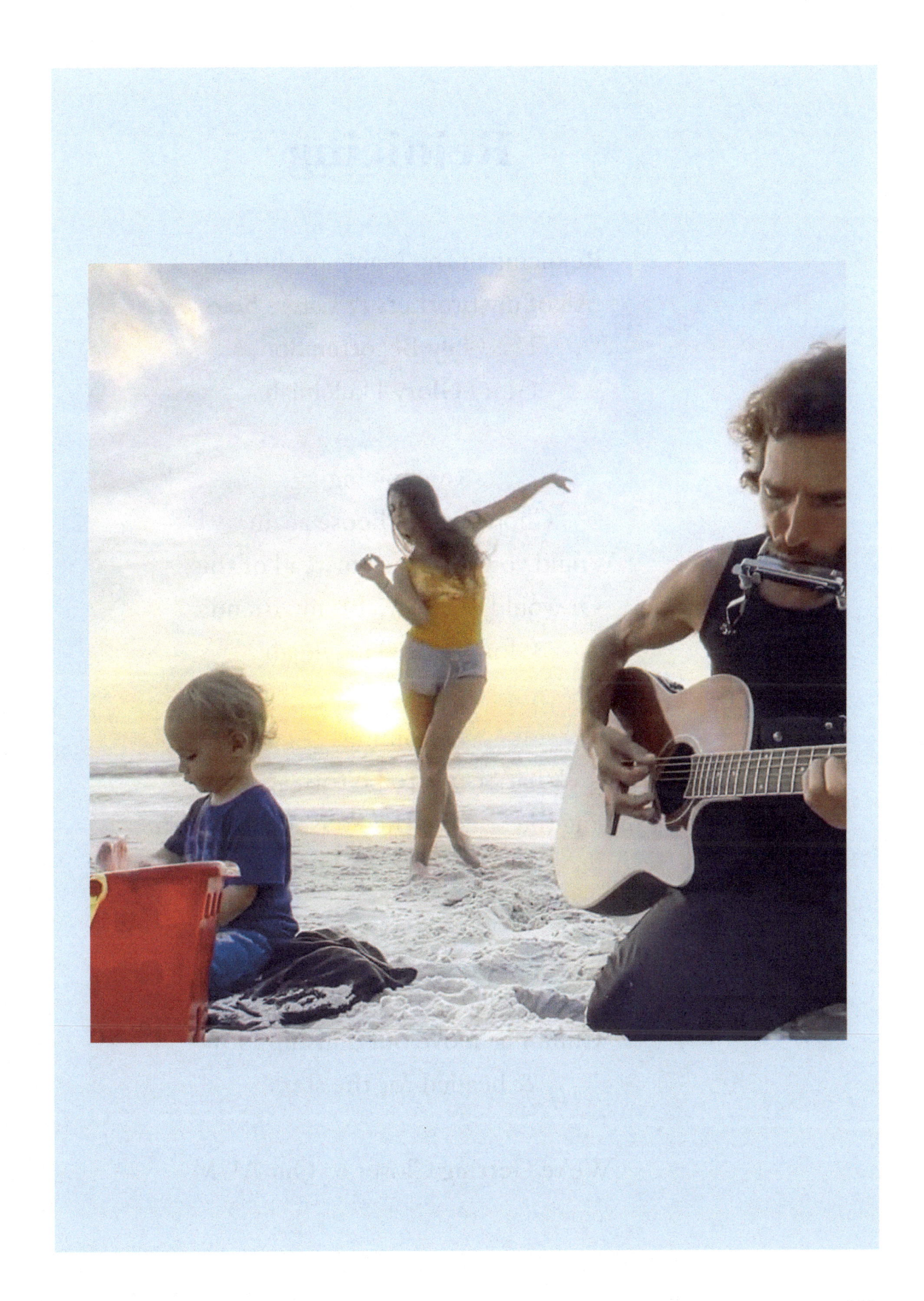

Rejoicing

Rejoicing in the Name of the One
All of my brothers & sisters here
The Only Begotten Son
Glory Glory Hallelujah

Re-choicing
Choosing to choose again
Would you see peace instead of this,
Or would you be right, my friend?
Glory Glory Hallelujah

Rejoining
What Seems to be torn apart
Singing the Song of the Sonship now with
One Love, One Heart

Rejoicing
In the Name of the One
Climbing above our Sunship Now
& headed for the stars

We're Getting Closer to Our AUM

Your Grace is Given Me

Your grace is given me
I claim it now
Father, I come to you
& you come to me
I am the son you love
The son you love

This grace I give to thee
Will you claim it now
Mama, I come to you
Will you come, too?

You are the one I love
The one I love

Spirit is in a state of grace forever
Our reality is only spirit
We are in that state of grace forever & ever

Let's end all our grieving
Self-deceiving
Blind believing
'cause life is for living
& love is forgiving

This grace I give to thee
Will you claim it now?

"Together we go, or not at all."

Happy Song

♪♪♪

When you're down, when you're sad
try singin' a happy song
'cause maybe life ain't so so bad
When you're singin' a happy song

Happy Song, baby
Happy Song – hey give it a try!

I just don't
wanna see
Nobody cry

When life's a'thumpin' all around
Don't get left out in the cold
Don't let your troubles bring ya down
& don't put your life on hold
'Cause the show must go
the show must go
the show must go on...
So strike up the band!
& come on and sing that happy song

Happy Song, baby
Happy Song – hey give it a try!
Ah just don't
Wanna hear
Nobody sigh
♪♪♪

Breathe

Breathe
Breathe in the air
Breathe
Breathe in the air
Try not to care
We're almost there
Breathe in the air

Breathe
Breathe in the sun
Breathe
Breathe in the sun
Come to the one
We've just begun
Breathe in the sun

Breathe
Just Breathe
Breathe
Just Breathe
You don't have to believe
You just have to breathe
Just Breathe

Breathe
Breathe in the air
Breathe
Breathe in the air
Try not to care
We're already there

The Greeting
Helen Schucman

Say but "I love you"
to all living things,
And they will lay their blessing over you
To keep you ever safe
and ever sure
That you belong to God
and He to you.

What but "I love you" could the greeting be
Of Christ to Christ,
Who welcomes but Himself?
And what are you except the Son of God,
The Christ
Whom He would welcome to Himself?

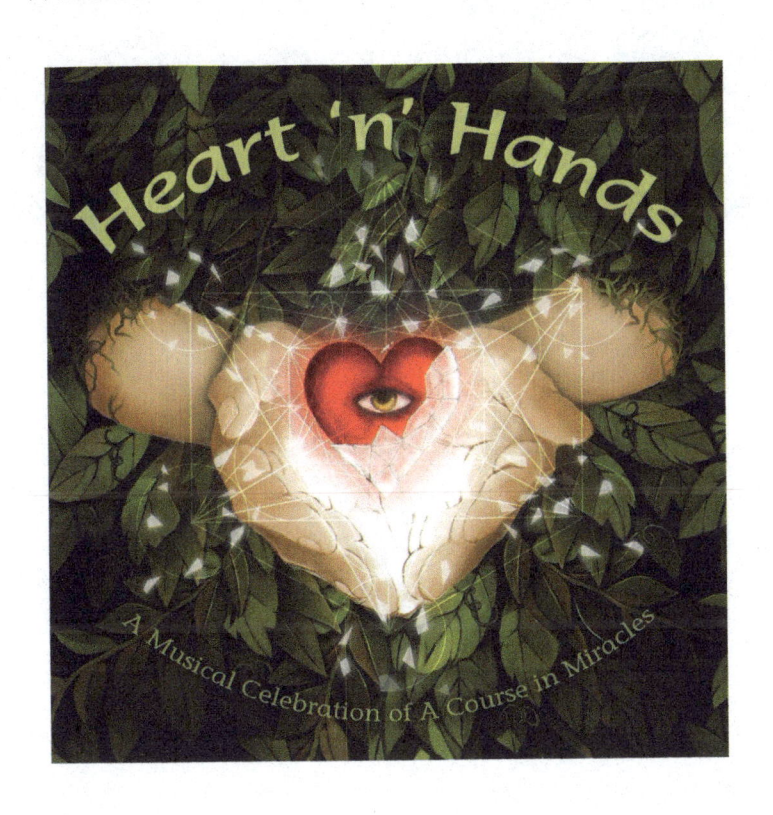

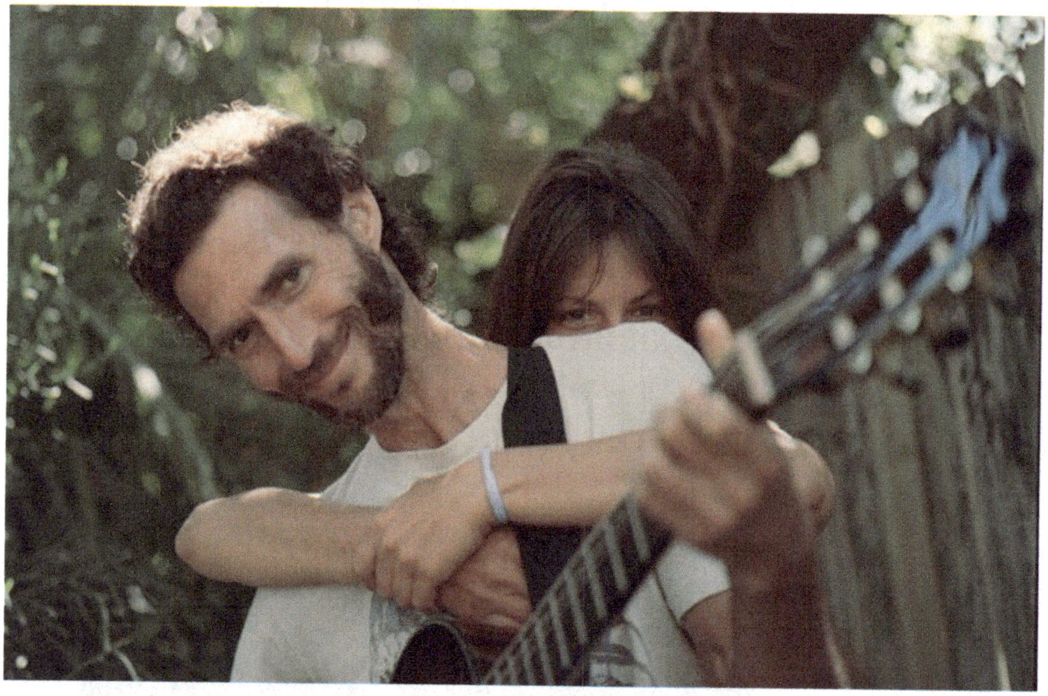

When Will There Be Peace on Earth?

POEMS

Look to This Day

Look to this day:
For it is life, the very life of life.
In its brief course
Lie all the verities and realities of your existence.
The bliss of growth,
The glory of action,
The splendour of achievement
Are but experiences of time.

For yesterday is but a dream
And tomorrow is only a vision;
And today well-lived, makes
Yesterday a dream of happiness
And every tomorrow a vision of hope.
Look well therefore to this day;
Such is the salutation to the ever-new dawn!

~ Kalidasa

Wean Yourself

Little by little, wean yourself.
This is the gist of what I have to say.
From an embryo, whose nourishment
comes in the blood,
move to an infant drinking milk,
to a child on solid food,
to a searcher after wisdom,
to a hunter of more invisible game.

Think how it is to have a conversation
with an embryo.
You might say, "The world outside is vast
and intricate.
There are wheatfields and mountain
passes,
and orchards in bloom.

At night there are millions of galaxies, and
in sunlight
the beauty of friends dancing at a
wedding."

You ask the embryo why he, or she, stays
cooped up
in the dark with eyes closed.

Listen to the answer.

There is no "other world."
I only know what I've experienced.
You must be hallucinating."

~ Rumi

Awake to the Name

To be born in a human body is rare,
Don't throw away the reward of your past good deeds.
Life passes in an instant—
the leaf doesn't go
back to the branch.
The ocean of rebirth sweeps up all beings hard,
Pulls them into its cold-running,
fierce, implacable currents.
Giridhara, your name is the raft,
the one safe-passage over.
Take me quickly.
All the awake ones travel with Mira, singing the name.
She says with them: Get up, stop sleeping—
the days of a life are short.

- Mirabai

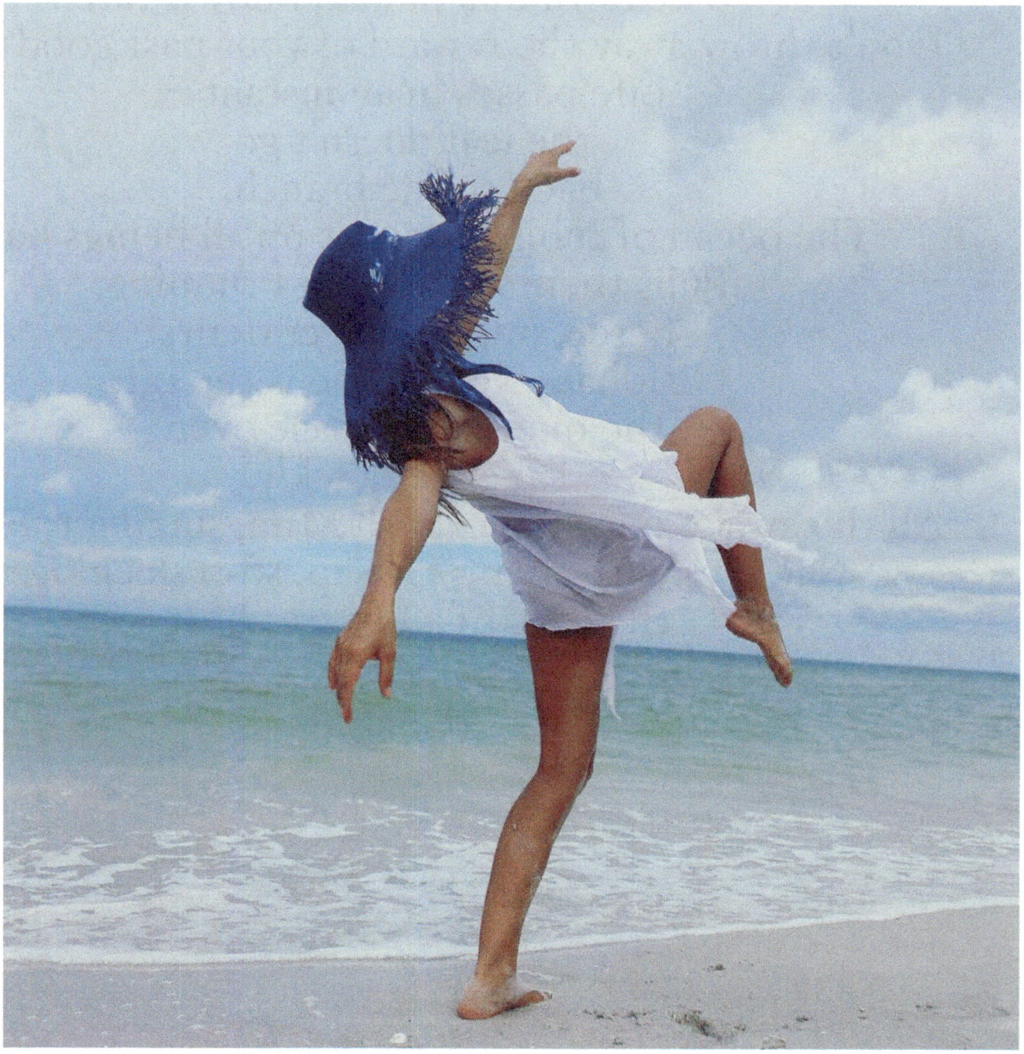

Quest for God

O'ver hill and dale and mountain range,
In temple, church, and mosque,
In Vedas, Bible, Al Koran
I had searched for Thee in vain.

Like a child in the wildest forest lost
I have cried and cried alone,
"Where art Thou gone, my God, my love?
The echo answered, "gone."

And days and nights and years then passed
A fire was in the brain,
I knew not when day changed in night
The heart seemed rent in twain.
I laid me down on Ganges's shore,
Exposed to sun and rain;
With burning tears I laid the dust
And wailed with waters' roar.

I called on all the holy names
Of every clime and creed.
"Show me the way, in mercy, ye
Great ones who have reached the goal."

Years then passed in bitter cry,
Each moment seemed an age,
Till one day midst my cries and groans
Some one seemed calling me

A gentle soft and soothing voice
That said 'my son' 'my son',
That seemed to thrill in unison
With all the chords of my soul.
I stood on my feet and tried to find
The place the voice came from;
I searched and searched and turned to see
Round me, before, behind,
Again, again it seemed to speak
The voice divine to me.
In rapture all my soul was hushed,
Entranced, enthralled in bliss.
A flash illumined all my soul;
The heart of my heart opened wide.
O joy, O bliss, what do I find!
My love, my love you are here
And you are here, my love, my all!

And I was searching thee -
From all eternity you were there
Enthroned in majesty!
From that day forth, wherever I roam,
I feel Him standing by
O'ver hill and dale, high mount and vale,
Far far away and high.

The moon's soft light, the stars so bright,
The glorious orb of day,
He shines in them; His beauty - might -
Reflected lights are they.
The majestic morn, the melting eve,
The boundless billowing sea,
In nature's beauty, songs of birds,
I see through them - it is He.

When dire calamity seizes me,
The heart seems weak and faint,
All nature seems to crush me down,
With laws that never bend.
Meseems I hear Thee whispering sweet
My love, "I am near", "I am near".
My heart gets strong. With thee, my love,
A thousand deaths no fear.
Thou speakest in the mother's lay
Thou shuts the babies eye,
When innocent children laugh and play,
I see Thee standing by.

When holy friendship shakes the hand,
He stands between them too;
He pours the nectar in mother's kiss
And the baby's sweet "mama".
Thou wert my God with prophets old,
All creeds do come from Thee,
The Vedas, Bible, and Koran bold
Sing Thee in Harmony.

"Thou art," Thou art" the Soul of souls
In the rushing stream of life.
"Om tat sat om." Thou art my God,
My love, I am thine, I am thine.

~Swami Vivekananda

TAKE PEACE, TAKE HEAVEN

PRAYER OF FRA GIOVANNI GIOCONDO
A Letter to the Most Illustrious the *Contessina Allagia Dela Aldobrandeschi*, written Christmas Eve, *Anno Domini 1513*.

I am your friend, and my love for you goes deep.
There is nothing I can give you which you do not already
possess. However, there is much, very much that, while I
cannot give it, you can take!

No heaven can come to us unless our hearts
find rest in it today. Take heaven!

No peace lies in the future which is not hidden in this
present little instant. Take peace!

The gloom of the world is but a shadow.
Behind it, yet within our reach, is joy.
There is radiance and glory in darkness,
could we but see, and to see
we have only to look. I beseech you to look.

Life is so generous a giver, but we,
judging its gifts by their covering,
cast them away as ugly or heavy or hard.

Remove the covering and you will find beneath it
a living splendor, woven of love, by wisdom,
with power.

Welcome it, grasp it, and you touch
the angel's hand that brings it to you.

Everything we call a trial, a sorrow, or a duty,
believe me, that angel's hand is there.

The gift is there, and the wonder
of an overshadowing presence.

Our joys, too - be not content with them as joys.
They, too, conceal diviner gifts.

Life is so full of meaning and purpose,
so full of beauty beneath its surface,
that you will find that earth but cloaks
your heaven. Courage then, to claim it.
That is all!

But courage you have, and the knowledge
that we are pilgrims together,
wending home through an unknown country.

And so, at this time, I greet you!
Not quite as the world sends greetings
but with profound esteem, and with the prayers that for you
now and forever, the day breaks,
and shadows flee away.

~ Fra Giovanni

Simply Do This...
Hold Onto Nothing

Simply do this:

Be still, and lay aside all thoughts of what you are
and what God is;
all concepts you have learned about the world;
all images you hold about yourself.

Empty your mind of everything it thinks is either
true or false, or good or bad,
of every thought it judges worthy,
and all the ideas of which it is ashamed.

Hold onto nothing.

Do not bring with you one thought the past has taught,
nor one belief you ever learned before from anything.

Forget this world, forget this course,
and come with wholly empty hands unto your God."

~ A Course In Miracles

TOMORROW NEVER KNOWS
(Sir Lennon)

D -> C

Turn off your mind, relax and float downstrea
It is not dying, it is not dying

Lay down all thoughts, surrender to the void
It is shining, it is shining

That you may see the meaning of within
It is being, it is being

That love is all and love is everyone
It is knowing, it is knowing

That ignorance and hate may mourn the dead
It is believing, it is believing

But listen to the colour of your dreams
It is not living, it is not living

Or play the game "Existence" to the end
Of the beginning, of the beginning
Of the beginning, of the beginning
Of the beginning, of the beginning

Brahman

The Luminous Brahman dwells in the cave of the heart and is known to move there. It is the great support of all;
for in It is centered everything that moves, breathes and blinks.
O disciples, know that to be your Self—that which is both gross and subtle, which is adorable, supreme and beyond the understanding of creatures.
(2.2.1)

That which is radiant, subtler than the subtle,
That by which all the worlds and their inhabitants are supported—
That, verily, is the indestructible Brahman;
That is the prana, speech and the mind;
That is the True and That is the Immortal.
That alone is to be struck.
Strike It, my good friend. (2.2.2)
Take the Upanishad as the bow,
the great weapon and place upon it the arrow sharpened by meditation.
Then, having drawn it back with a mind directed to the thought of Brahman,
strike that mark, O my good friend—that which is the Imperishable. (2.2.3)

Aum is the bow; the atman is the arrow;
Brahman is said to be the mark.
It is to be struck by an undistracted mind.
Then the atman becomes one with Brahman, as the arrow with the target.
(2.2.4)

In Him are woven heaven, earth, and the space between, and the mind with all the sense-organs.
Know that non-dual Atman alone and give up all other talk.
He is the bridge to Immortality. (2.2.5)
He moves about, becoming manifold, within the heart,
where the arteries meet, like the spokes fastened in the nave of a chariot wheel. Meditate on Atman as Aum. Hail to you!
May you cross beyond the sea of darkness! (2.2.6)

He who knows all and understands all
and to whom belongs all the glory in the world—
He, Atman, is placed in the space in the effulgent abode of Brahman.
He assumes the forms of the mind and leads the body and the senses.

He dwells in the body, inside the heart.
By the knowledge of That which shines as the blissful and immortal Atman,
the wise behold Him fully in all things. (2.2.7)
The fetters of the heart are broken, all doubts are resolved
and all works cease to bear fruit, when He is beheld who is both high and low. (2.2.8)
There the stainless and indivisible Brahman shines in the highest, golden sheath.
It is pure; It is the Light of lights; It is That which they know who know the Self. (2.2.9)

The sun does not shine there, nor the moon and the stars, nor these lightnings,
not to speak of this fire. When He shines, everything shines after Him;
by His light everything is lighted. (2.2.10)
That immortal Brahman alone is before, that Brahman is behind,
that Brahman is to the right and left.
Brahman alone pervades everything above and below;
this universe is that Supreme Brahman alone. (2.2.11)

~ Mandukya Upanishad
(Yogananda translation)

The Invitation

It doesn't interest me what you do for a living.

I want to know what you ache for, and if you dare to dream of meeting your hearts longing.

It doesn't interest me how old you are. I want to know if you will risk looking like a fool for love, for your dreams, for the adventure of being alive.

It doesn't interest me what planets are squaring your moon. I want to know if you have touched the center of your own sorrow, if you have been opened by life's betrayals, or have become shriveled and closed from fear of further pain.

I want to know if you can sit with pain, mine or your own, without moving to hide it or fade it or fix it.
I want to know if you can be with joy, mine or your own; if you can dance with wildness and let the ecstasy fill you to the tips of your fingers and toes without cautioning us to be careful, be realistic, or to remember the limitations of being human.

It doesn't interest me if the story you are telling me is true, I want to know if you can disappoint another to be true to yourself.

If you can bear the accusation of betrayal and not betray your own soul.

I want to know if you can be faithful and therefore trustworthy. I want to know if you can see beauty,

even when it is not pretty every day, and if you can source your life from its presence.

I want to know if you can live with failure, yours or mine, and still stand on the edge of a lake and shout to the silver of the full moon,

"Yes!"

It doesn't interest me to know where you live or how much money you have. I want to know if you can get up after the night of grief and despair, weary and bruised to the bone, and do what needs to be done for the children.

It doesn't interest me who you are, or how you came to be here- I want to know if you will stand in the center of the fire with me and not shrink back.

It doesn't interest me where or what or with whom you have studied I want to know what sustains you from the inside when all else falls away. I want to know if you can be alone with yourself, and if you truly like the company you keep in the empty moments.

~ Oriah Mountain Dreamer, Indian Elder

What If?

What if our religion was each other?

If our practice was our life?

If prayer was our words?

What if the Temple was the Earth?

If forests were our church?

If holy water—the rivers, lakes and oceans?

What if meditation was our relationships?

If the Teacher was life?

If wisdom was self-knowledge?

If love was the center of our being

~ Ganga White

Akla Cholo Re

If there is no-one responding to your call - then go on all alone

If no-one speaks (to you), don't think you are unfortunate,
if no-one speaks (to you),

If everyone turns away, if everyone fears (to speak),
then with an open heart without hesitation
speak your mind alone

If everyone walks away, O unlucky one, everyone walks away

If no-one looks back towards the (your) unpredictable path,
then with thorn pricked (of the path) bloodied feet, walk alone

If no-one heeds your call - then walk alone

If no-one shines a light (on the path, O unlucky one,

If the dark night brings a storm at the door - then let the lightning
ignite the light in you alone to shine on the path

If no-one heeds your call - then walk alone

- Rabindranath Tagore

The Way of the Warrior

The Way of the Warrior is simple, my dear ones. However, it may be simple but it's not always easy. Today I would like to give you a few of my simple guidelines or "rules of the road", if you will. And that road is the Way of the Warrior.

The Warrior always speaks her truth – no matter what the circumstances.

The Warrior is totally detached from what others think and say about her. [This is absolutely necessary if she's going to observe the first rule above.]

The Warrior always does her best to see the Divinity in all that is. In this way, she shall never have any desire to own, control, manipulate, misuse or abuse any of the Great Spirit's creatures.

The Warrior always follows the highest path as dictated by the highest authority in the universe – herself.

The Warrior totally trusts in – and surrenders to – the flow of her life. She knows all is as it should be. Therefore, she must always completely trust in – and surrender to – her higher Self, her Soul, the Great Spirit.

The Warrior knows all Love, all Wisdom, all Power lie within her – within her mind, her body, her heart, her Soul. There is nothing to seek, nothing to find, nowhere to go – except WITHIN.

The Warrior knows with absolute certainty she has never made a mistake – she can never make a mistake. All of her life is simply a lesson in this classroom called planet Earth. She learns as she goes.
All is as it should be.

The Warrior never takes life on planet Earth too seriously. It's all a game, after all – a game in the classroom of planet Earth. And games should be fun. Enjoy the game – it won't last forever!

The Warrior's heart is always full – and always grateful. She never knows lack or emptiness – except, that is, when she creates those illusions by getting too infatuated with the Great Illusion – the human experience.

The Warrior knows the Great Illusion creates some highly interesting challenges – for example, the challenge to rise above the Great Illusion.

As she rises above the Great Illusion, the Warrior knows this experience is as it should be – she has chosen it. And in this choosing, she is remembering her way back to the Light – back to her Home. That was the only reason for choosing the Great Illusion in the first place.

The Warrior knows all her brothers and sisters on planet Earth have the same destination she does – HOME. But each may take a different path. And the Warrior knows that's okay! All will get Home – no matter what path they take. It cannot be otherwise – for ALL paths lead Home.

The Warrior knows the way of the wind. She loves the wind, but she knows she cannot capture it – she cannot own it. She can love it, luxuriate in its presence, glory in its energy. But if she tries to capture it, it becomes something other than what it truly is – it becomes still and stagnant air.

She can never possess it completely – unless she refuses to ever own it – unless she refuses to ever have sovereignty over it. She can possess it only by letting it be free – by letting it be what it is.

It cannot be otherwise.

The Way of the Warrior is the Way of the Wind.

~ Chief Joseph

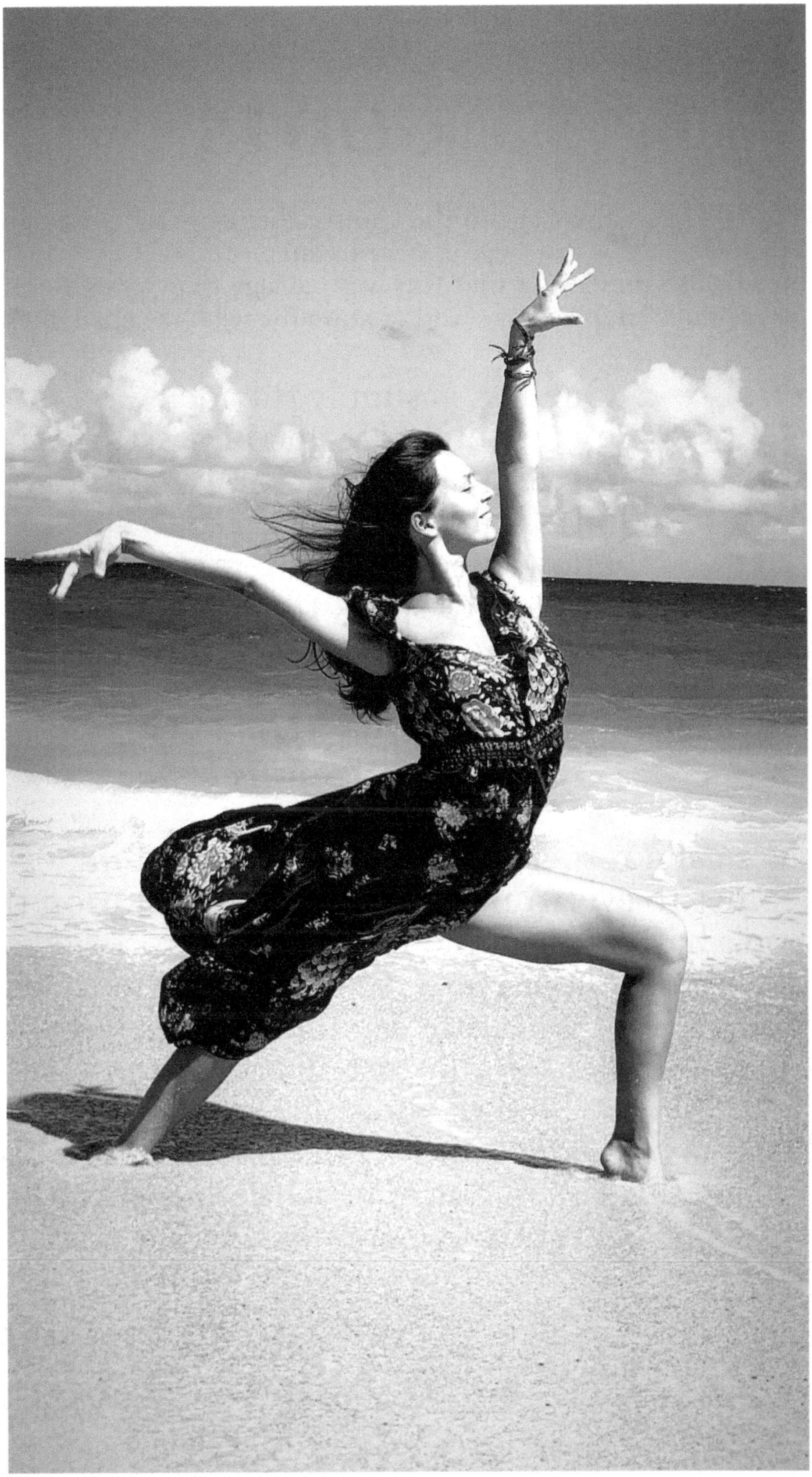

GOD IS

[Note: This is a passage in the Course that directly connects with Helen's dream.
You will also remember that this was passage that we earlier changed to read "Love" in place of "God" – and now we have changed it back.]

Oneness is simply the idea God is.
And in His Being, He encompasses all things.
No mind holds anything but Him.
We say "God is," and then we cease to speak, for in that knowledge words are meaningless.
There are no lips to speak them, and no part of mind sufficiently distinct to feel that it is now aware of something not itself.
It has united with its Source. And like its Source Itself, it merely is.

We cannot speak nor write nor even think of this at all.
It comes to every mind when total recognition that its will is God's has been completely given and received completely.
It returns the mind into the endless present, where the past and future cannot be conceived.
It lies beyond salvation; past all thought of time, forgiveness and the holy face of Christ.
The Son of God has merely disappeared into his Father, as his Father has in him. The world has never been at all.
Eternity remains a constant state.

- A Course in Miracles

*"By our fruits they shall know us,
& we shall know ourselves."*

The Beatitudes

*"Blessed are the poor in spirit,
for theirs is the kingdom of heaven.*

*Blessed are they who mourn,
for they shall be comforted.*

*Blessed are the meek,
for they shall inherit the earth.*

*Blessed are they who hunger and thirst for righteousness,
for they shall be satisfied.*

*Blessed are the merciful,
for they shall obtain mercy.*

*Blessed are the pure of heart,
for they shall see God.*

*Blessed are the peacemakers,
for they shall be called children of God.*

*Blessed are they who are persecuted for the sake of righteousness,
for theirs is the kingdom of heaven."*

~ Gospel of St. Matthew 5:3-10

Samadhi

Vanished the veils of light and shade,
Lifted every vapor of sorrow,
Sailed away all dawns of fleeting joy,
Gone the dim sensory mirage.
Love, hate, health, disease, life, death:
Perished these false shadows on the screen of duality.
The storm of maya stilled
By magic wand of intuition deep.
But ever-present, all-flowing I, I, everywhere.
Planets, stars, stardust, earth,
Volcanic bursts of doomsday cataclysms,
Creation's molding furnace,
Glaciers of silent X-rays, burning electron floods,
Thoughts of all men, past, present, to come,
Every blade of grass, myself, mankind,
Each particle of universal dust,
Anger, greed, good, bad, salvation, lust,
I swallowed, transmuted all
Into a vast ocean of blood of my own one Being.
Smoldering joy, oft-puffed by meditation
Blinding my tearful eyes,
Burst into immortal flames of bliss,
Consumed my tears, my frame, my all.
Thou art I, I am Thou,
Knowing, Knower, Known, as One!
Tranquilled, unbroken thrill,
eternally living, ever-new peace.

Enjoyable beyond imagination of expectancy, samadhi bliss!
Not an unconscious state
Or mental chloroform without willful return,
Samadhi but extends my conscious realm

Beyond the limits of the mortal frame
To farthest boundary of eternity
Where I, the Cosmic Sea,
Watch the little ego floating in Me.
Mobile murmurs of atoms are heard,
The dark earth, mountains, vales, lo! molten liquid!
Flowing seas change into vapors of nebulae!
Aum blows upon vapors, opening wondrously their veils,
Oceans stand revealed, shining electrons,
Till, at the last sound of the cosmic drum,
Vanish the grosser lights into eternal rays
Of all-pervading bliss.
From joy I came, for joy I live, in sacred joy I melt.
Ocean of mind, I drink all creation's waves.
Four veils of solid, liquid, vapor, light,
Lift aright.
I, in everything, enters the Great Myself.
Gone forever: fitful, flickering shadows of mortal memory;
Spotless is my mental sky, below, ahead, and high above;
Eternity and I, one united ray.
A tiny bubble of laughter, I
Am become the Sea of Mirth Itself.

~ Paramahamsa Yogananda

Nirvana

All is abolished but the mute Alone.

The mind from thought released, the heart from grief,
Grow inexistent now beyond belief;

There is no I, no Nature, known-unknown.

The city, a shadow picture without tone,

Floats, quivers unreal; forms without relief
Flow, a cinema's vacant shapes; like a reef
Foundering in shoreless gulfs the world is done.

Only the illimitable Permanent
Is here.

A Peace stupendous, featureless, still.

Replaces all, – what once was I, in It
A silent unnamed emptiness content
Either to fade in the Unknowable
Or thrill with the luminous seas of the Infinite.

~ Sri Aurobindo

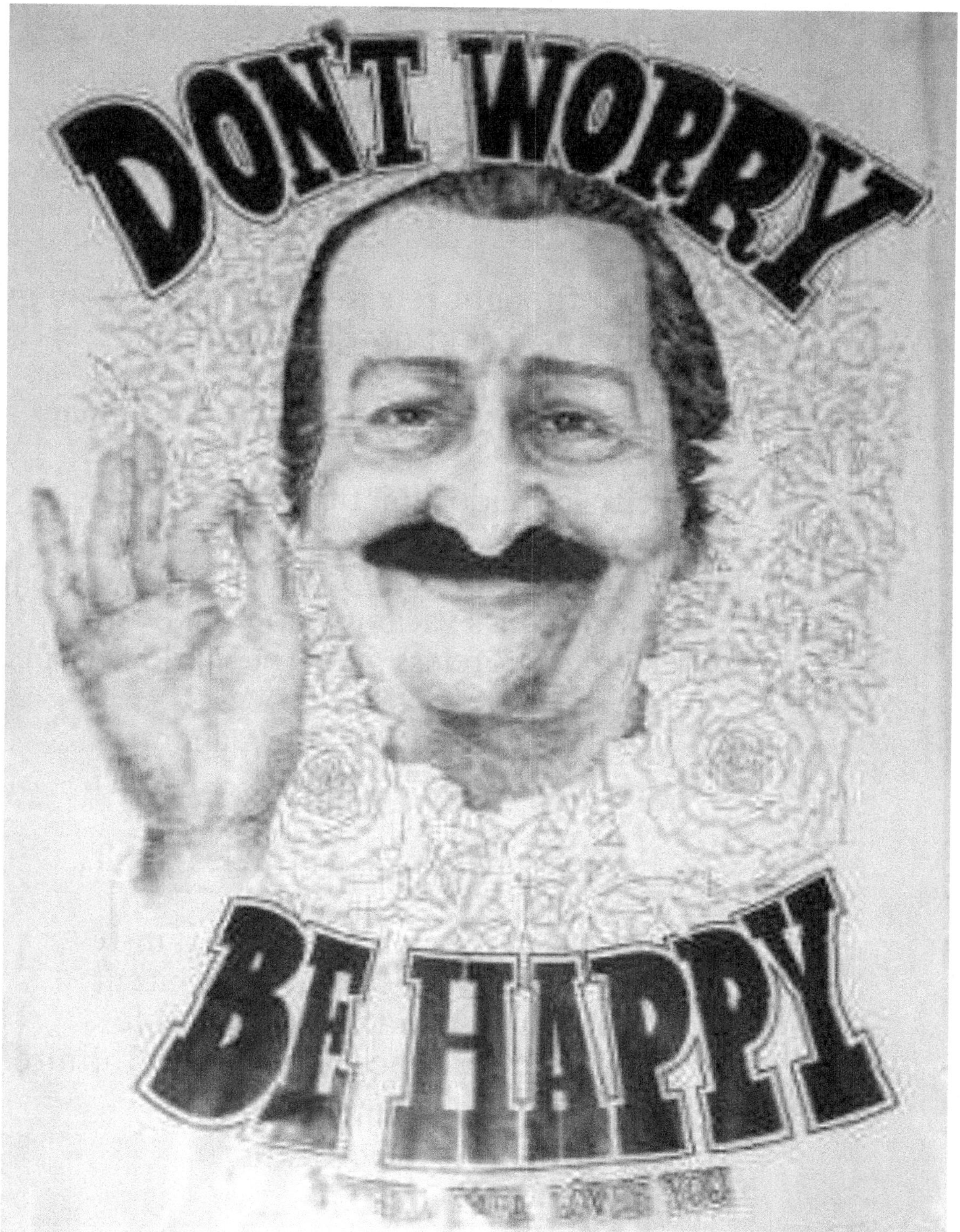
DON'T WORRY
BE HAPPY

The Master's Prayer

O Parvardigar, the Preserver and Protector of All,
You are without Beginning and without End,
Non-dual, beyond comparison,

and none can measure You.

You are without colour, without expression,

without form and without attributes.

You are unlimited and unfathomable, beyond imagination and conception,
eternal and imperishable.

You are indivisible,

and none can see You but with eyes Divine.

You always were, You always are, and You always will be.

You are everywhere; You are in everything;
and You are also beyond everywhere and beyond everything.

You are in the firmament and in the depths.

You are manifest and unmanifest on all planes and beyond all planes;
You are in the three worlds and also beyond the three worlds.

You are imperceptible and independent.

You are the Creator, the Lord of Lords, the Knower of all minds and hearts;
You are Omnipotent and Omnipresent.

You are Knowledge Infinite, Power Infinite and Bliss Infinite.

You are the Ocean of Knowledge, All-knowing,

Infinitely-knowing,
the Knower of the past, the present, and the future;
and You are Knowledge itself.

You are All-merciful and eternally benevolent.

You are the Soul of souls, the One with infinite attributes.

You are the Trinity of Truth, Knowledge and Bliss;
You are the Source of Truth, the Ocean of Love.

You are the Ancient One, the Highest of the High;
You are Prabhu and Parameshwar;
You are the Beyond-God

and the Beyond-Beyond-God also;

You are Parabrahma, Allah, Elahi, Yezdan, Ahuramazda, and God the Beloved.

You are named Ezad: the only One worthy of worship.

~ Meher Baba

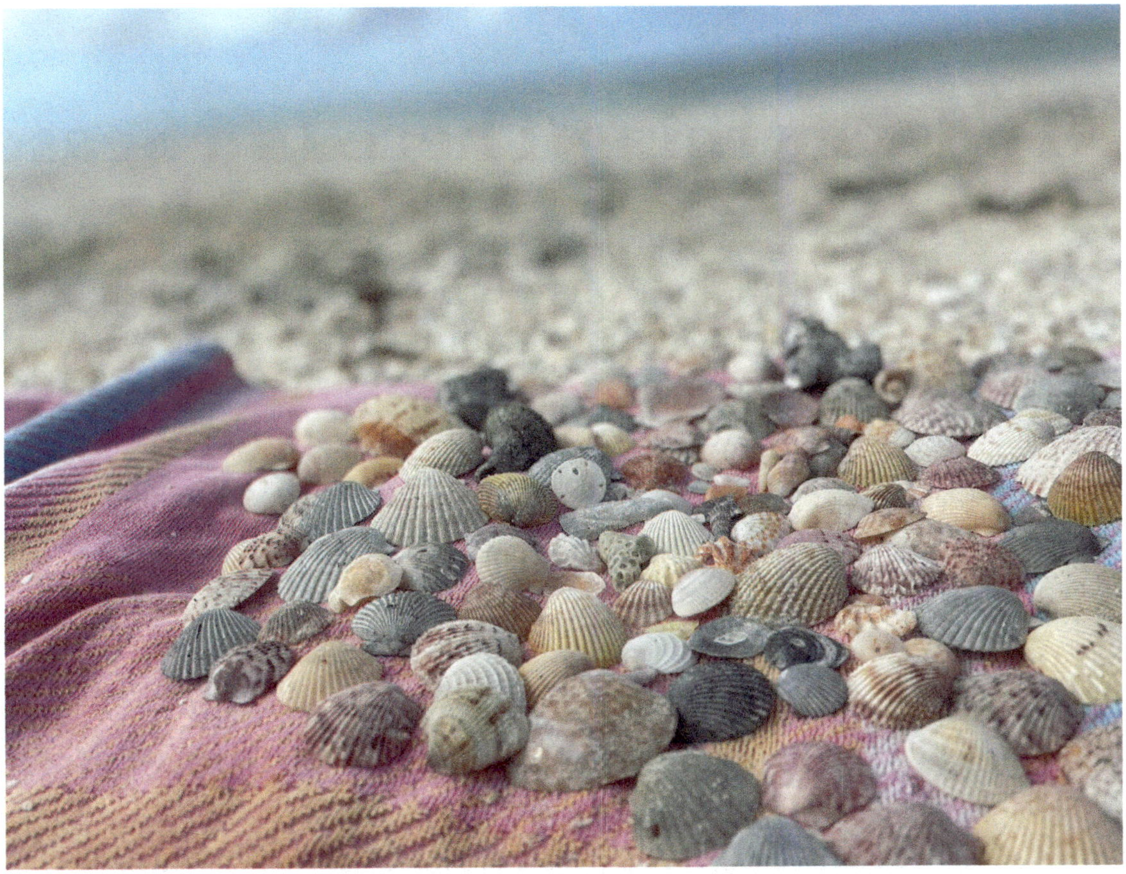

To Everything There Is a Season

To everything there is a season,
And a time to every purpose under heaven:
A time to be born, and a time to die;
A time to plant, and a time to pluck up that which is planted;
A time to kill, and a time to heal;
A time to break down, and a time to build up;
A time to weep, and a time to laugh;
A time to mourn, and a time to dance;
A time to cast away stones,

and a time to gather stones together;
A time to embrace, and a time to refrain from embracing;
A time to get, and a time to lose;
A time to keep, and a time to cast away;
A time to rend, and a time to sew;
A time to keep silence, and a time to speak;
A time to love, and a time to hate;
A time of war, and a time of peace.

~ **Ecclesiastes** 3:1-8

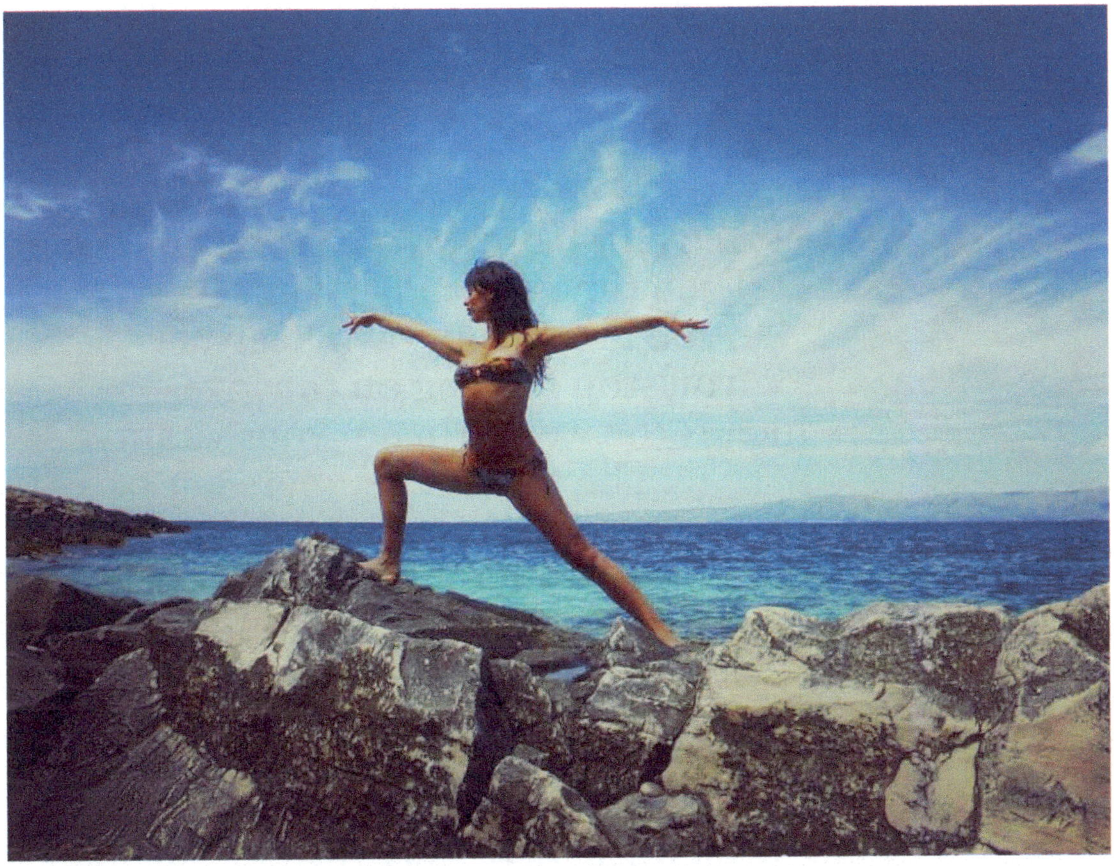

Judge Not Yourself

My beloved child, break your heart no longer.
Each time you judge yourself,
you break your own heart;
you stop feeding on the love
which is the wellspring of your vitality.
The time has come.
Your time to live, to celebrate.
And to see the goodness that you are.
You, my child, are Divine.
You are pure.
You are sublimely free.
You are God in disguise
and you're always perfectly safe.
Do not fight the dark, just turn on the light.
Let go and Breathe into the Goodness that you are.

~ Swami Kripalu

Nirvana-Shatakam
Six Verses on Liberation

mano-buddhyahaṅkāra-cittā ni nāhaṁ na ca śrotrajihve na ca ghrāṇanetre |
na ca vyoma-bhūmiḥ na tejo na vāyuḥ cidānandarūpaḥ śivo'haṁ śivo'haṁ ||

I am not mind, nor intellect, nor ego, nor feeling-consciousness (citta).

I am not touch, hearing, taste, smell nor sight (the five senses).

I am not ether, earth, radiance (fire), nor air (the five elements).

I am conscious bliss in form, I am Spirit, I am Spirit.

na ca prāṇasañjño na vai pañcavāyuḥna vā saptadhātur na vā pañcakośaḥ |
na vāk pāṇipādau na copasthapāyū cidānandarūpaḥ śivo'haṁ śivo'haṁ ||

I am not life-force (prāṇa), nor the five breaths (vāyus),

nor the seven bodily metals, nor the five sheaths of consciousness (kośa).

Not the bodily functions of elimination, procreation, motion,

holding, or speaking.

I am conscious bliss in form, I am Spirit, I am Spirit.

na me dveṣa-rāgau na me lobha-mohau mado naiva me naiva mātsarya-bhāvaḥ |
na dharmo nacārtho na kāmo na mokṣaḥ cidānandarūpaḥ śivo'haṁ śivo'ham ||

I have no aversion nor attraction to anything, no greed,

nor delusion, nor ego-pride, nor envy.

Not duty (dharma), nor wealth, nor desire, nor liberation (mokṣa).

I am conscious bliss in form, I am Spirit, I am Spirit.

na puṇyaṁ na pāpaṁ na saukhyaṁ na duḥkhaṁ na mantro na tīrthaṁ na vedā na yajñāḥ |
ahaṁ bhojanaṁ naiva bhojyaṁ na bhoktā cidānandarūpaḥ śivo'haṁ śivo'ham ||

Not virtue, nor vice, not happiness nor sadness.

No mantras, holy places, scriptures (Vedas), nor rituals (yajña).

I am not the one who eats food, nor the act of eating, nor the food itself.

I am conscious bliss in form, I am Spirit, I am Spirit.

na me mṛtyuśaṅkā na me jātibhedaḥ pitā naiva me naiva mātā na janma |
na bandhur na mitraṁ gurur-naiva śiṣyaḥ cidānandarūpaḥ śivo'haṁ śivo'ham ||

For me there is no death nor identification with caste.

I have no father, nor mother, nor birth.

Not relatives, nor friends, nor guru, nor students.

I am conscious bliss in form, I am Spirit, I am Spirit.

ahaṁ nirvikalpo nirākāra-rūpo vibhur-vyāpya sarvatra sarvendriyāṇām |
sadā me samatvaṁ na muktir na bandhaḥ cidānandarūpaḥ śivo'haṁ
śivo'ham ||

I am without any attributes and without any form.

I am all-pervading, omnipresent, eternal.

I am beyond both liberation (mukti) and material bondage.

I am conscious bliss in form, I am Spirit, I am Spirit.

~ *Adi Shankarcharya*

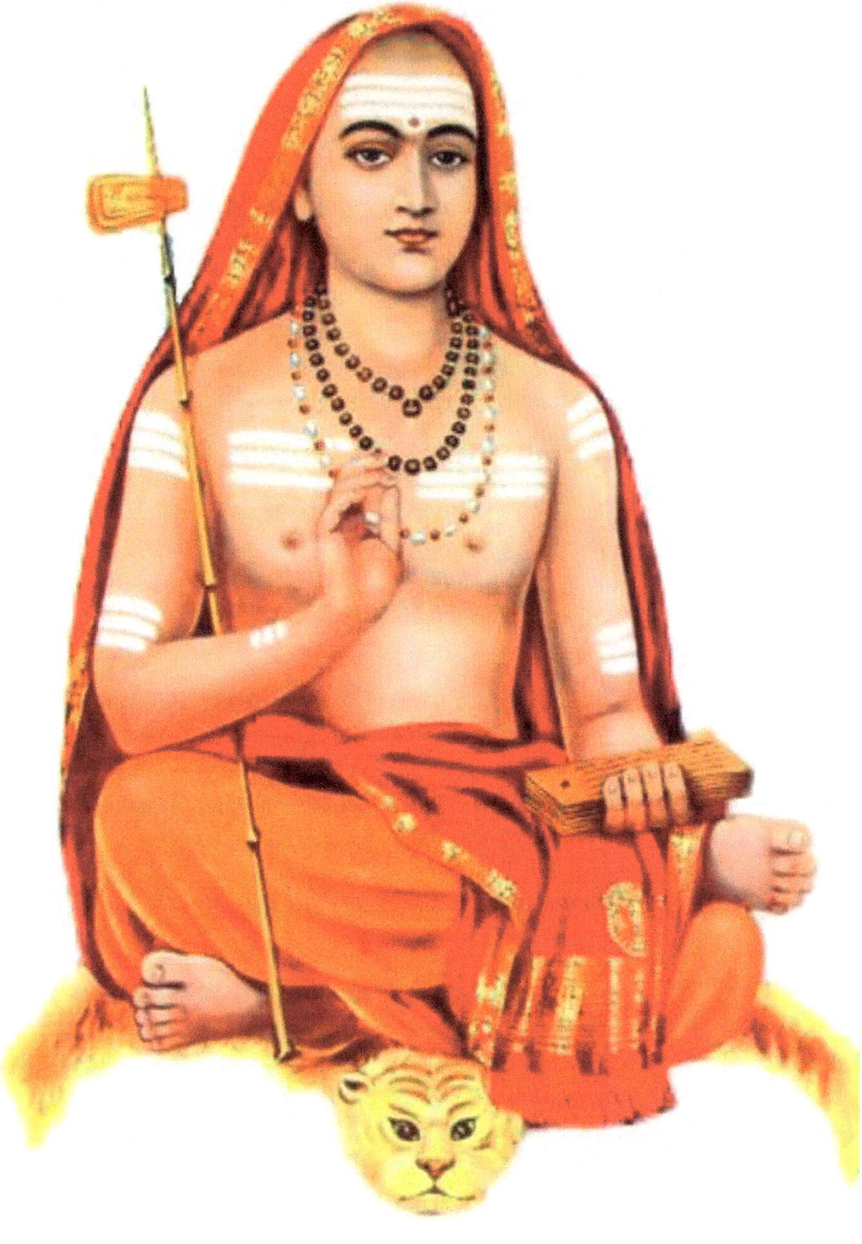

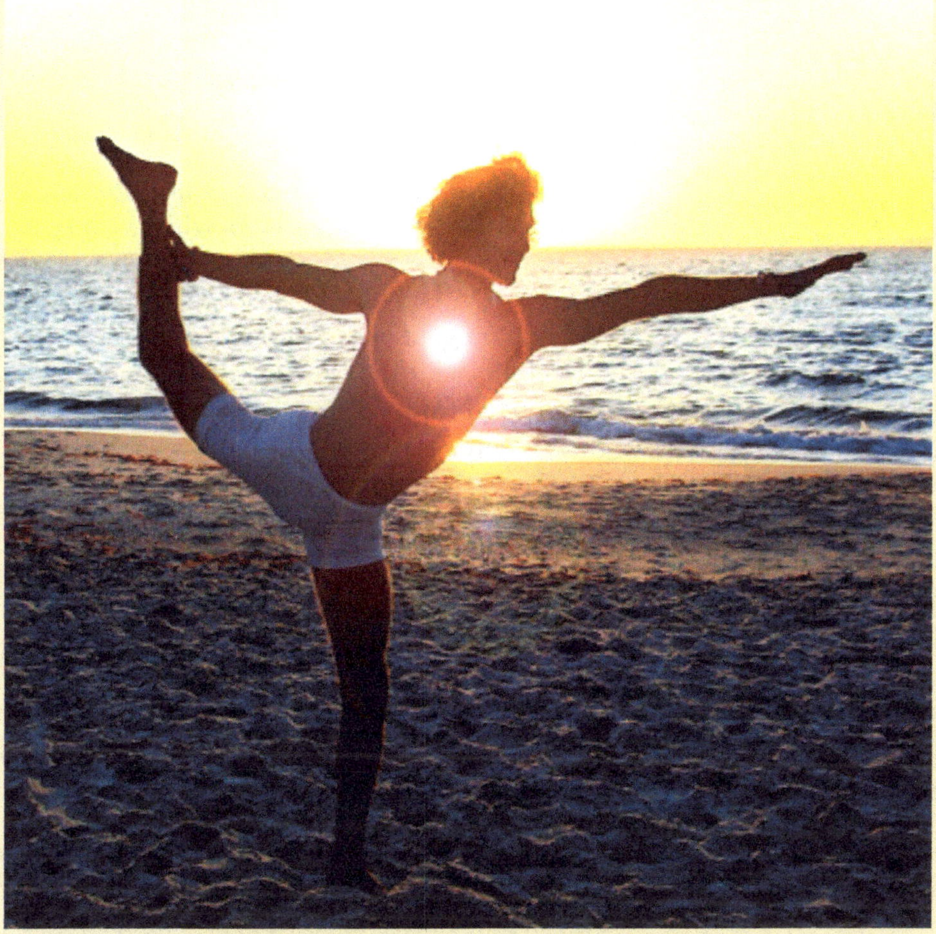

Yoga Means Union

Yoga,
Yoga means Union --
Peelin' back the layers of the onion
Tears keep falling from my eyes
As I see where the ego's truth lies
a flimsy disguise
But I know in the end there's gonna be a Pearl
Janus Girl, no more world in a whirl...

Yoga,
Yoga means Union
Reelin' back the layers of opinion
(no need for a minyan, minions)
Towards the final consensus:
CommUniSon
No more neMesis, brosis
The truth right under our gnosis
Just The Universe as Mighty ChorUs
Self-proclaiming the OneLoveness <3

Sometimes I think yoga is boring
But then I say to myself,
"Nah, am-a-stay"
(_/_NAMASTE _/_)
I'm gonna stay here in my heart
& live the part
never meant to live in some *apart*-ment
what comes and goes
came and went
I'm only here to re-*present*...

Yoga,
Yoga Just Is
Says what it means
& means what it says.
& it's gleaning is just around the bend --
the end to the means
and the means to
The End

~ Allowah

I Follow the Religion of Love

*My heart holds within it every form...
it contains a pasture for gazelles,
a monastery for Christian monks.
There is a temple for idol-worshippers,
a holy shrine for pilgrims;
There is the table of the Torah,
and the Book of the Koran.
I follow the religion of Love
and go whichever way His camel leads me.
This is the true faith;
This is the true religion.*

~ Ibn Arabi

Beyond the Body

Beyond the body, beyond the sun and stars, past everything you see and yet somehow familiar, is an arc of golden light that stretches as you look into a great and shining circle. And all the circle fills with light before your eyes. The edges of the circle disappear, and what is in it is no longer contained at all. The light expands and covers everything, extending to infinity forever shining and with no break or limit anywhere. Within it everything is joined in perfect continuity. Nor is it possible to imagine that anything could be outside, for there is nowhere that this light is not.

She Let Go

She let go.
She let go. Without a thought or a word, she let go.
She let go of the fear.
She let go of the judgments.
She let go of the confluence of opinions swarming around her head.
She let go of the committee of indecision within her.
She let go of all the 'right' reasons.
Wholly and completely, without hesitation or worry,

she just let go.

She didn't ask anyone for advice.
She didn't read a book on how to let go.
She didn't search the scriptures.

She just let go.

She let go of all of the memories that held her back.
She let go of all of the anxiety that kept her from moving forward.
She let go of the planning and all of the calculations about how to do it just right.
She didn't promise to let go.
She didn't journal about it.
She didn't write the projected date in her Day-Timer.
She made no public announcement and put no ad in the paper.
She didn't check the weather report or read her daily horoscope.

She just let go.

She didn't analyze whether she should let go.
She didn't call her friends to discuss the matter.
She didn't do a five-step Spiritual Mind Treatment.
She didn't call the prayer line.
She didn't utter one word.

She just let go.

No one was around when it happened.
There was no applause or congratulations.
No one thanked her or praised her.
No one noticed a thing.
Like a leaf falling from a tree, she just let go.
There was no effort.
There was no struggle.
It wasn't good and it wasn't bad.
It was what it was, and it is just that.
In the space of letting go, she let it all be.
A small smile came over her face.
A light breeze blew through her.
And the sun and the moon shone forevermore…

~ Safire Rose

As I Began to Love Myself ~

A Poem on Self Love

As I began to love myself I found that anguish and emotional suffering are only warning signs that I was living against my own truth. **Today, I know, this is AUTHENTICITY.**

As I began to love myself I understood how much it can offend somebody. As I try to force my desires on this person, even though I knew the time was not right and the person was not ready for it, and even though this person was me.
Today I call it RESPECT.

As I began to love myself I stopped craving for a different life, and I could see that everything that surrounded me was inviting me to grow.
Today I call it MATURITY.

As I began to love myself I understood that at any circumstance, I am in the right place at the right time, and everything happens at the exactly right moment. So I could be calm.
Today I call it SELF-CONFIDENCE.

As I began to love myself I quit steeling my own time, and I stopped designing huge projects for the future.
Today, I only do what brings me joy and happiness, things I love to do and that make my heart cheer, and I do them in my own way and in my own rhythm.
Today I call it SIMPLICITY.

As I began to love myself I freed myself of anything that is no good for
my health – food, people, things, situations, and everything that drew me down and away from myself. At first I called this attitude a healthy egoism. **Today I know it is LOVE OF ONESELF.**

As I began to love myself I quit trying to always be right, and ever since
I was wrong less of the time. **Today I discovered that is MODESTY.**

As I began to love myself I refused to go on living in the past and worry
about the future. Now, I only live for the moment, where EVERYTHING
is happening. **Today I live each day, day by day, and I call it FULFILLMENT.**

As I began to love myself I recognized that my mind can disturb me and it can make me sick. But As I connected it to my heart, my mind became a valuable ally. **Today I call this connection WISDOM OF THE HEART.**

We no longer need to fear arguments, confrontations or any kind of problems with ourselves or others.
Even stars collide, and out of their crashing new worlds are born.
Today I know that this LIFE.

Author - The origin of this poem is uncertain. It is believed to have been written by *Charlie Chaplin on his 70th birthday, however some give credit to Kim & Alison McMilen, for a poem titled, "When I Loved Myself Enough".

~ Charlie Chaplin

Love

I have loved Thee with two loves –

a selfish love and a love that is worthy of Thee.

As for the love which is selfish,

Therein I occupy myself with Thee,
to the exclusion of all others.

But in the love which is worthy of Thee,
Thou dost raise the veil that I may see Thee.

Yet is the praise not mine in this or that,
But the praise is to Thee in both that and this.

~ Rabia al Basri

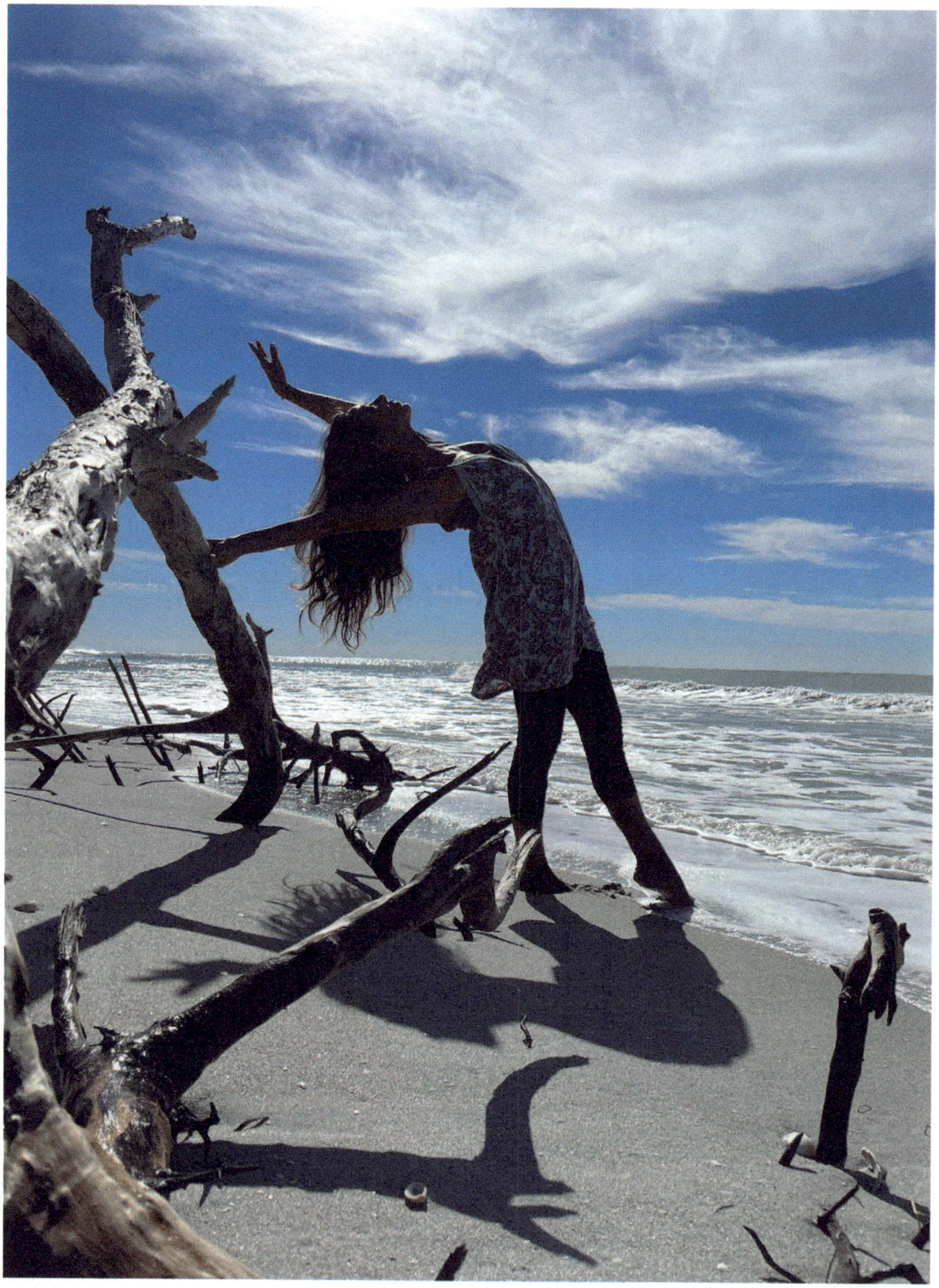

Sri Atma Gita

Om Sri Atma Gita now I'll sing~On hearing which a man is freed~That heart receptive to God's word~Becomes the Lord Hari's abode~

On the wheel of change a man is turned~Until Sri Atma Gita's heard~Even the place in which it's sung~Becomes a sacred place of Love~

Oh man, seek thee the highest goal~Read or sing this song each day~True understanding thou wilt gain~And all past sins will fade away~

To one who hears this song at death~Sri Krishna out of love bestows~A place on high and those who give~This song as a gift are One with Him~

Om O souls who yearn for truth~Come sip Sri Krishna's honeyed word~Who hears this song is freed from death~ And gains the precious peace of God~

O noble Uddhava, remember my words~For I'll not be around to remind you again~Give up all attachment, surrender your love~ For this world of sense-objects relations, and friends~

*The feeling of "i" as a separate self~**must be given up if you wish to know truth**~There's only one "Self" which exists within all~'Tis this very Self that you see as the world~*

The Self is the source of the whole Universe~ It fashions all forms of it's own Consciousness ~Though all forms are changing and soon fade away~The one conscious Self is forever the same~

Therefore Uddhava, cling fast to the Self~Your mind must be steady, unswayed by the world~Your heart must be free of all selfish desire~If you wish to awake and to know who you are~

When you have gained knowledge and wisdom as well~When you can feel one with the whole universe~When ypu've found the Self and in Self found delight~Then you will be free, though you live still on earth~

Thus will you go beyond evil and good~With out pride or shame you'll be have as you should~To everyone Loving and Gentle and Kind~

You'll see not but One and in One keep your mind~

Oh Krishna my God, only Soul of the world ~So that I may awake please instruct me still more~My mind is so dull I'm unable to see~The way that a man from his flesh can be free~

Listen Uddhava, take refuge in me~Perform all your duties and works faithfully~But keep your heart free from all want or desire~And surrender your heart and your mind unto me~

This world which the senses perceives is a dream~There's nothing within it that is what it seems~So keep your mind steady, remembering me~And do what you must while your heart remains free~

To work with the motive of pleasing oneself~Leads only to ruin and darkness within~But the works that are done in the service of God~Bring freedom and peace as the fruits of reward

With your mind wide awake and remembering me ~ Surrender all thought of yourself and be free~

give up the false notion of '"myself and "my own" ~ Become one with God through devotional love~

Regard all your brothers with equality ~ See only oneself in whatever you see ~ With all doubts dispelled by the bright light of truth ~Awake from the dream of this world and be free ~

When you've become free of all worldly desire ~ No power and can shake you or move you to ire ~ Unstirred by the words of both good men and bad ~ Uddhava, be free, keep your mind fixed on God ~

O Krishna, all men are aware that the world~ Is changing and fleeting, a whirlpool of dust ~ Yet see how all men run to fill their desires ~ See how they're caught in the jaws of dark lust ~

Though suffering and misery runs after those men ~ Who seek for their pleasure the objects of sense~ Please tell me, dear

Krishna, why it should be so ~ That men, like dumb beasts love their suffering so~

Uddhava, such poor men do not know the truth ~ Nor have they the peace and contentment that comes ~ From know the bliss of the one conscious Self ~ Pervading this world in these myriad forms ~

Such men are deluded in thinking the Self ~ Is body and mind and the organs of sense ~ Betrayed by desires of the flesh they are led ~ By dreams of sense-pleasure until they are dead ~

By giving himself to the impulse of lust ~ A foolish man gathers up pain for himself ~ But a man of dispassion and knowledge is wise ~ He gathers the fruits of a joy that's divine ~

So listen Uddhava, give up lethargy ~ Keep watch on the thoughts of your mind faithfully ~ Withdraw your regard from the world and it's play ~ Remember the Self with each thought every day ~

"Tis this which is known as the yoga supreme ~ I've taught it to god's and I've taught it to men ~ I'll tell you Uddhava the words which I gave ~To the great sage Sanaka in a far-distant age ~

The question Sanaka asked of me was this: ~ "The mind is attracted to objects of sense ~ And objects of sense become fixed in the mind ~ How can I be free from sense objects that bind" ~

What you say is true I assured him at once ~ But your niether mind nor the objects of sense ~ There's only one "I" ever free and divine ~ When you know that Self then true freedom you'll find ~

That vision that sees many where there is one ~ Is sleep though one's eyes may appear open wide ~ The one conscious Self is the Reality ~ Awake from the dream of this world and be free ~

Dispell the dark clouds of delusion with truth ~ With knownledge and wisdom shed light on the Self ~ Realize who you are and by knowledge be freed ~ Devotion to truth is the true love indeed ~

Today the world is but, tomorrow it's not ~ It sifts like the forms of the clouds in the sky ~ It is but one Consciousness seeming to be ~The manifold world which the senses perceive ~Withdraw from this world of appearance your mind ~ And give up the thirst for the pleasures of life - With mind set at rest know the bliss of the Self - And never more fall into error and strife -

That man who has tasted the bliss of the Self - May move among objects of sense without fear - His mind never clings to the world's misery - His heart is with God and his mind is made free -

This is the secret Sanaka was taught - The goal of all men and the highest of paths - Give worship to God as the Self of your heart - See only one Self and remain unattached -

Dear Krishna the sages have taught many ways - To reach to the end of man's journey to God - I wish to know, Lord, the way that is best - Can each of these ways be as good as the rest -

Uddhava my child, there are many ways - Which sages have shone to attain the Supreme - The pathways are many and each of them leads - To the knowledge of God beyond scriptures or creeds -

By love, or by inward control of the mind - By faith, or by wisdom, by serving mankind - All these have been taught as the way to reach God - But the best way of all is devotional love -

What joy does one find in the sweet love of God - The bliss of his love fills the whole universe - Uddhava delight in that Lord who's within

Surrender your life in devotion to Him - As wood is burnt up when it's thrown into fire -

Devotional love burns up worldly desire. - By study of books man may try to find joy - But, God who is Love is found only through love. - Without love for God all man's learning is vain -

"Tis only through love that true bliss is regained - With joy in his heart that wise lover is blessed - Who serves God with Love; - 'tis this path which is best -

Uddhava, obtain that sweet blessing of grace - By taking the path that is followed by saints - Give worship to God through devotional hymns - Perform all your actions in service to Him -

Be free from all selfish desires of the mind - Renounce everything for the love that's divine - When your mind is surrendered and evermore true - That love which is bliss will awaken in you -

This goal is the highest goal one can attain - God's freedom and bliss in the form of a man - All pleasure, all knowledge, all power divine - Belongs to that man who's surrendered the mind -

So therefore Uddhava, restrain the desire - For outward enjoyments through organs of sense - And trun your mind inward with love to the Self - Through deep meditation regain your true wealth -

Learn to be even in mind and in poise - Be calm in the midst of the mightiest storm - Though men may upbraid you and call you false names - Remember the Self, remain ever the same -

Do not allow hatred to rise up in you - Nor ever in anger return blow for blow - But keep your mind turned to the Self who's within - And strive to be free from the bondage of sin -

O Master, dear teacher, O Soul of the world - When one is insulted and false words are hurled - How hard is the task of remaining in peace - Please show me the way I can do this with ease -

Indeed it is true there's nothing more hard - The words of the wicked strike deep in the heart - Like arrows they lodge in the breast of a man - And Cause such a pain that he hardly can stand -

But please let me tell you, Uddhava my child, - A story of one who was painfully tried - By torment and mis'ry throughout all his life - Yet ever remain free of pain and of strife -

This man was once wealthy and foolishly proud - 'Til fate intervened and deprived him of all - But the blow fortune dealt him was good in disguise - For he soon realized where man's real treasure lies -

With his mind turned within he examined his soul - While wond'ring the earth as a sudhu alone - Though poor in the eye of all men of the world - He soon became wealthy in trus self-control -

Now other men saw him alone and detached - And desided to test him by treating him rough - Wherever he went he was treated with scorn - As men tried to wound him with words and with stones -

But though he was treated by all men with spite - The truth of the Self he kept ever in sight - Tormented incessantly, injured and wronged - He sang in his heart this pain-dispelling song -

"No pleasure, No pain can affect my true Self - Both suff'ring and pleasure belong to the mind - The Self is the witness of all the mind's play - Remaining forevermore conscious and free. -

The Self, like an object reflected in glass - Appears to be mind and the whole universe - And man, by forgetting his identity - Is lost in delusion and knows misery -

All teaching's of sages have one common goal - They all teach the way to attain self-control - The highest religion consists of just this: - To Bridle the mind and in truth become fixed -

The uncontrolled mind is man's sole evil foe - It vanquishes men with it's weapons of woe - Forgetful of this men see evil in men - Like fools, they forget that all evil's within -

None other can cause me to know joy or pain - For I am forever the unchanging One - The sense of delight or of sadness I find - Comes from the false notion that I am the mind -

Awake to the knowledge that God is your Self - Let all of your actions be guided by Him - Surrender your life in the service of God - And your heart will be filled with the light of His Love -

Take up your abode with the holiest saints - Those sages who's live's are devoted to God - And learn by their conduct to live as you must - To see only One in this vast universe -

Oh nobal Uddhava, your sight must be pure - To see only God in this manifold world - Such vision is wisdom that sets the soul free - See only one Consciousness incessantly -

By seeing in all men the spirit divine - The notion of 'others' abandons the mind - Realize this one truth and your heart will be free - Of anger and hatred and mean jealousy. -

That man who has seen God sees God everywhere ~ He worships the Self in all hearts as his own ~ This is the best mode of worship indeed ~ To treat all as God in one's thought, word, and deed ~

Such is the wisdom I pass on to you ~ By which in this life you may learn to be free ~ And loose all attachment to things passing by ~ And know your true Self as immortality ~

Dear Brother, said Suta, the tale has been told ~ Of Uddhava and Krishna in days long ago ~ The fountain of nectar which flowed from the lips ~ Of Sri Krishna enables all men to know bliss.~

I Bow to that Krishna, the one Soul of all ~ This song Atma Gita, His glory has told ~ May all men win freedom by singing this song ~ From the Srimad Bhagavatam Purana of old ~

~ Om Shanti Shanti Shanti Om ~

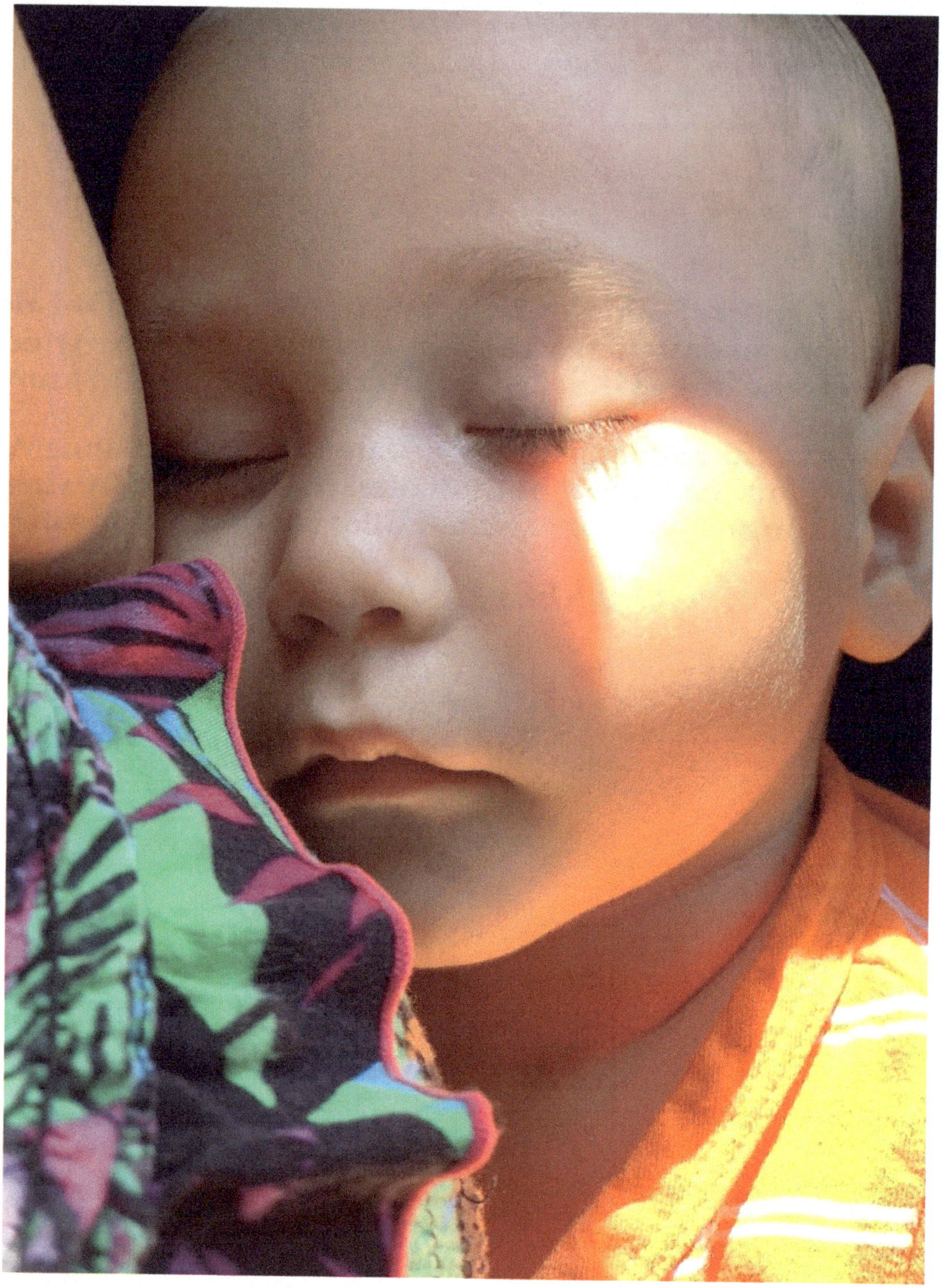

The Inner Ruler

All this is full. All that is full.
From fullness, fullness comes.
When fullness is taken from fullness,
Fullness still remains.
O M shanti shanti shanti

1. The Lord is enshrined in the hearts of all.
The Lord is the supreme Reality.
Rejoice in him through renunciation.
Covet nothing. All belongs to the Lord.

2. Thus working may you live a hundred years.
Thus alone will you work.

3. Those who deny the Self are born again
Blind to the Self, enveloped in darkness,
Utterly devoid of love for the Lord.

4. The Self is one. Ever still, the Self is
Swifter than thought, swifter than the senses.
Though motionless, he outruns all pursuit.
Without the Self, never could life exist.

5. The Self seems to move, but is ever still.
He seems far away, but is ever near.
He is within all, and he transcends all.

6. Those who see all creatures in themselves
And themselves in all creatures know no fear.

7. Those who see all creatures in themselves
And themselves in all creatures know no grief.
How can the multiplicity of life
Delude the one who sees its unity?

8. The Self is everywhere. Bright is the Self,
Indivisible, untouched by sin, wise,
Immanent and transcendent. He it is
Who holds the cosmos together.

9-11. In dark night live those for whom
The world without alone is real; in night
Darker still, for whom the world within
Alone is real. The first leads to a life
Of action, the second to a life of meditation.
But those who combine action with meditation
Cross the sea of death through action
And enter into immortality
Through the practice of meditation.
So have we heard from the wise.

12-14. In dark night live those for whom the Lord
Is transcendent only; in darker still,
For whom he is immanent only.
But those for whom he is transcendent
And immanent cross the sea of death
With the immanent and enter into
Immortality with the transcendent.
So have we heard from the wise.

15. The face of truth is hidden by your orb
Of gold, O sun. May you remove your orb
So that I, who adore the true, may see

16. The glory of truth. O nourishing sun,
Solitary traveler, controller,
Source of life for all creatures, spread your light
And subdue your dazzling splendor
So that I may see your blessed Self.
Even that very Self am I!

17. May my life merge in the Immortal
When my body is reduced to ashes.
O mind, meditate on the eternal Brahman.
Remember the deeds of the past.
Remember, O mind, remember.

18. O god of fire, lead us by the good path
To eternal joy. You know all our deeds.
Deliver us from evil, we who bow
And pray again and again.
O M shanti shanti shanti

~ Isha Upanishad

The Music Cannot Be Written

What is seen is not the Truth
What is cannot be said
Trust comes not without seeing
Nor understanding without words
The wise comprehends with knowledge
To the ignorant it is but a wonder
Some worship the formless God
Some worship His various forms
In what way He is beyond these attributes
Only the Knower knows
That music cannot be written
How can then be the notes
Says Kabir,
awareness alone will overcome illusion

- Kabir

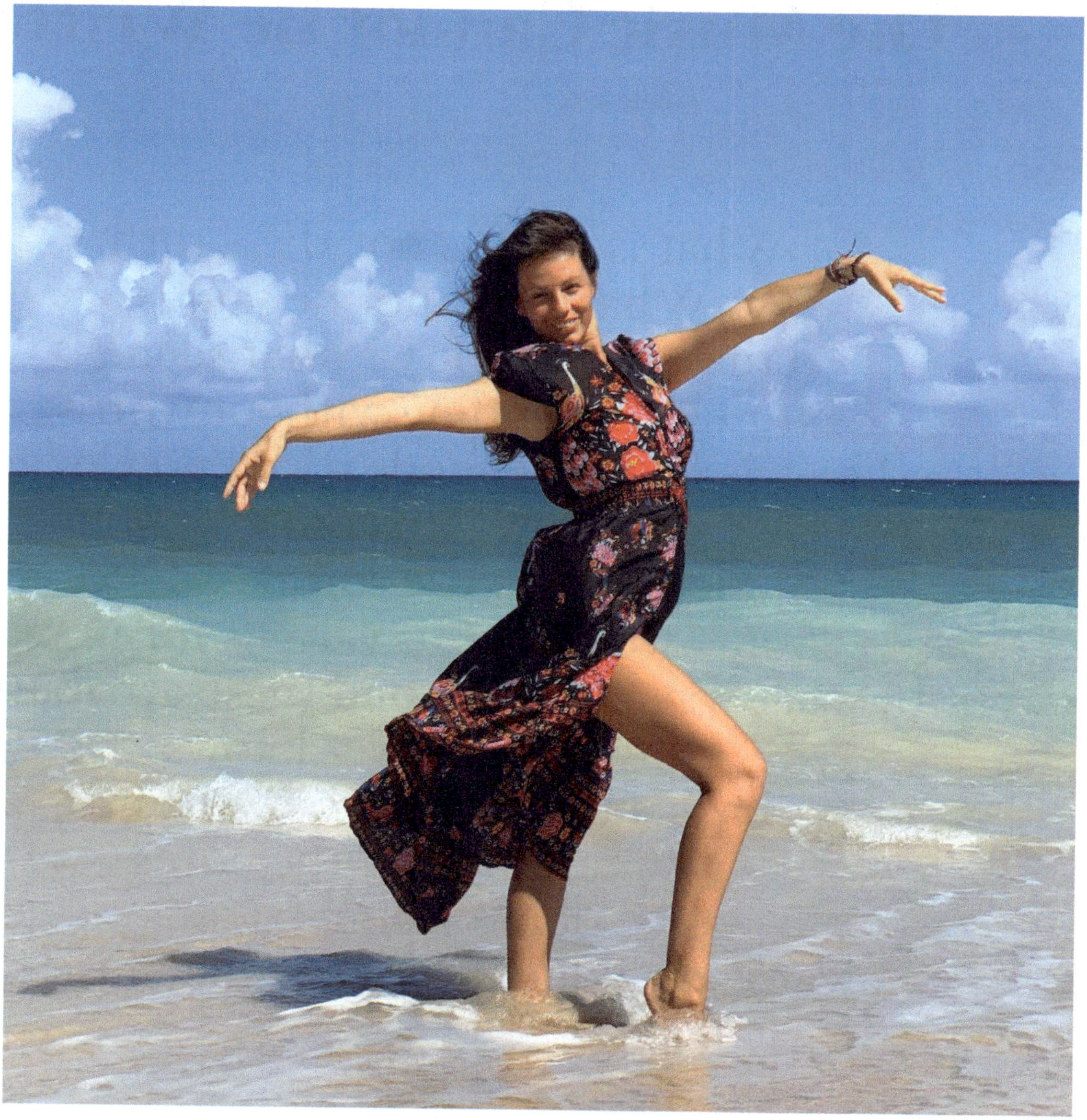

The Highest Bliss

But when he [Self] fancies that he is, as it were, a god,
or that he is, as it were, a king,
or "I am this altogether," that is his highest world,
This indeed is his (true) form, free from desires, free from evil, free from fear.

Now as a man, when embraced by a beloved wife,
knows nothing that is without, nothing that is within,
thus this person, when embraced by the *Prajna* (conscious, aware) Self,
knows nothing that is without, nothing that is within.
This indeed is his (true) form, in which his wishes are fulfilled,
in which the Self only is his wish, in which no other wish is left,
he is free from any sorrow.

Then a father is not a father, a mother not a mother,
the worlds not worlds, the gods not gods, the Vedas not Vedas.
Then a thief is not a thief, a murderer not a murderer,
a Sramana not a Sramana, a Tâpasa not a Tâpasa.
He is not affected by good, not affected by evil,
for he has then overcome all sorrows, all sufferings.
(...)
Thus did Yâgñavalkya teach him.
This is his highest Goal,
this is his highest Success,
this is his highest World,
this is his highest Bliss.

~ *Brihadaranyaka Upanishad*

Aham Prema

I am Love

LOVE NEVER FAILS

13 If I speak in the tongues[a] of men or of angels, but do not have love, I am only a resounding gong or a clanging cymbal.

2 If I have the gift of prophecy and can fathom all mysteries and all knowledge, and if I have a faith that can move mountains, but do not have love, I am nothing.

3 If I give all I possess to the poor and give over my body to hardship that I may boast,[b] but do not have love, I gain nothing.

4 Love is patient, love is kind. It does not envy, it does not boast, it is not proud.

5 It does not dishonor others, it is not self-seeking, it is not easily angered, it keeps no record of wrongs.

6 Love does not delight in evil but rejoices with the truth.

7 It always protects, always trusts, always hopes, always perseveres.

8 Love never fails. But where there are prophecies, they will cease; where there are tongues, they will be stilled; where there is knowledge, it will pass away.

9 For we know in part and we prophesy in part,

10 but when completeness comes, what is in part disappears.

11 When I was a child, I talked like a child, I thought like a child, I reasoned like a child. When I became a man, I put the ways of childhood behind me.

12 For now we see only a reflection as in a mirror; then we shall see face to face. Now I know in part; then I shall know fully, even as I am fully known.

13 And now these three remain: faith, hope and love.
But the greatest of these is love.
~ Corinthians

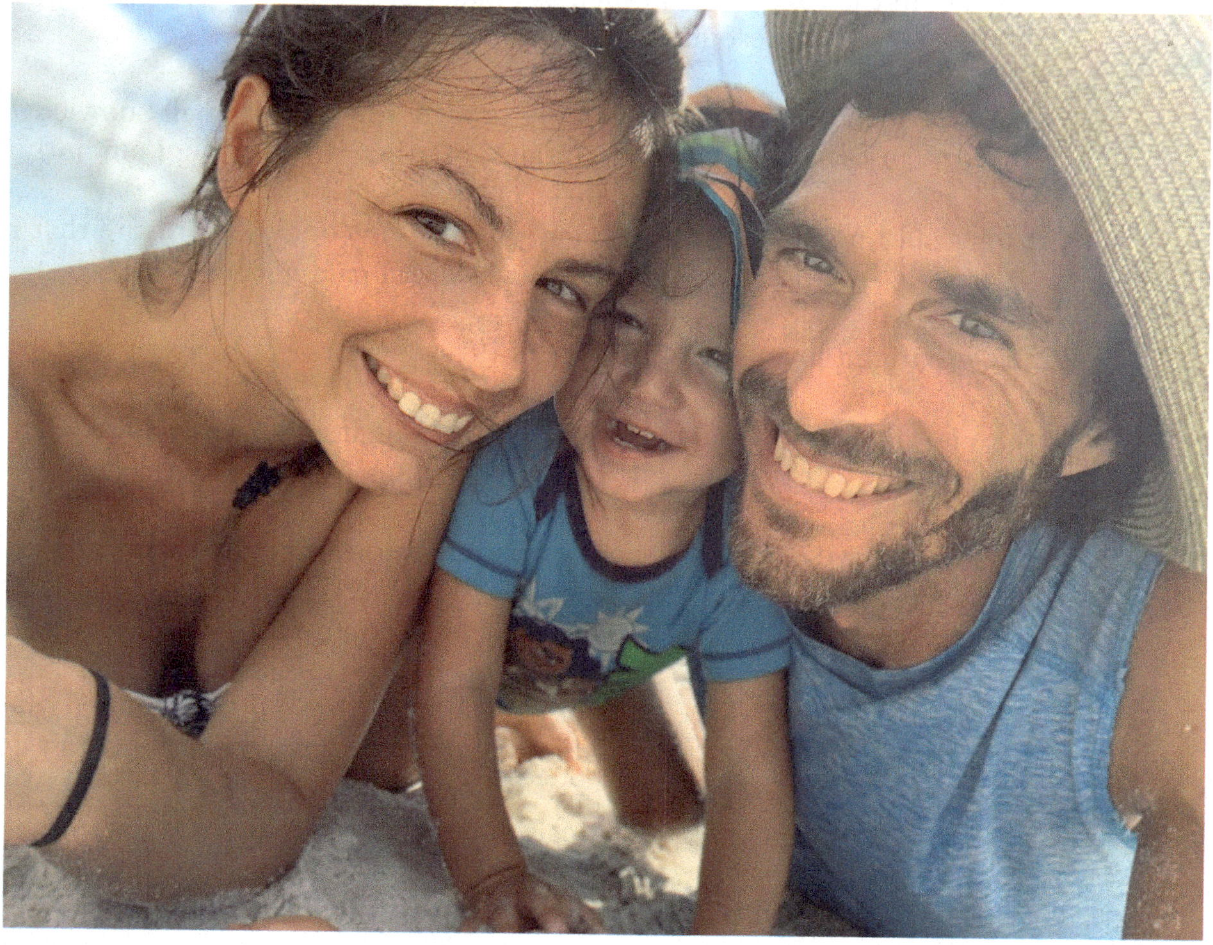

On Love

When love beckons to you, follow him,
Though his ways are hard and steep.
And when his wings enfold you yield to him,
Though the sword hidden among his pinions may wound you.
And when he speaks to you believe in him,
Though his voice may shatter your dreams
as the north wind lays waste the garden.

For even as love crowns you so shall he crucify you. Even as he is for your growth so is he for your pruning.
Even as he ascends to your height and caresses your tenderest branches that quiver in the sun,
So shall he descend to your roots and shake them in their clinging to the earth.

Like sheaves of corn he gathers you unto himself.
He threshes you to make you naked.
He sifts you to free you from your husks.
He grinds you to whiteness.
He kneads you until you are pliant;
And then he assigns you to his sacred fire, that you may become sacred bread for God's sacred feast.

All these things shall love do unto you that you may know the secrets of your heart, and in that knowledge become a fragment of Life's heart.

But if in your fear you would seek only love's peace and love's pleasure,
Then it is better for you that you cover your nakedness and pass out of love's

threshing-floor,
Into the seasonless world where you shall laugh, but not all of your laughter,
and weep, but not all of your tears.
Love gives naught but itself and takes naught but from itself.
Love possesses not nor would it be possessed;
For love is sufficient unto love.

When you love you should not say, "God is in my heart," but rather, "I am in
the heart of God."
And think not you can direct the course of love, for love, if it finds you worthy,
directs your course.

Love has no other desire but to fulfill itself.
But if you love and must needs have desires, let these be your desires:
To melt and be like a running brook that sings its melody to the night.
To know the pain of too much tenderness.
To be wounded by your own understanding of love;
And to bleed willingly and joyfully.
To wake at dawn with a winged heart and give thanks for another day of
loving;
To rest at the noon hour and meditate love's ecstasy;
To return home at eventide with gratitude;
And then to sleep with a prayer for the beloved in your heart and a song of
praise upon your lips.

~ Kahlil Gibran

OTHER TRULY HELPFUL OFFERINGS YOU MIGHT ENJOY...

About the WHO AM I? Series

The Who Am I? series is a trilogy of books that take the reader on an epic quest in search of the truth of existence.
They begin with "Who Am I" -- a book that looks searchingly into the question of what role and validity of psychedelics on the spiritual quest. The book is unique in that the author, Allowah, writes both from a trained academic perspective, and at the same time in an intentionally self-reflexive, expository way. The point being that we cannot separate the observer from the thing being observed, and it is also often helpful to see the author as a real person just like you, with similar challenges and struggles.

The second book in the series, "I Am Love," is very much an answer to the question posed in the first book, taking the reader deeper down the rabbit hole in the process of unraveling the mystery of consciousness. Whereas the first book was purposely ambivalent and open-ended, the second book is a bit more decided and prescriptive, though still cautiously so. And while the first book dealt more generally with psychedelics as a whole, the second book looks more specifically at Ayahuasca, which was only touched upon in the first volume. The second book also goes into much greater detail about the modern spiritual masterpiece *A Course in Miracles* and how it might be of assistance to those using Ayahuasca (or not) as a path to finding one's True Self -- the Self of All. The book is still quite reader-friendly, Allowah regularly dipping back into his own personal story to tell the greater tale, yet it is by no means as confessional and "tell-all" as the first book was.

It might be useful to see the first offering, "Who Am I?," as the Father; the second book, "I Am Love," as the Mother; and the third book in the series, "Love Is," as the child of the first two books. It is also the crest-jewel and the summation of the whole study, being one long meditation upon Love itself. It makes the point that while everyone knows what love is, nobody really knows what Love is, for the Love of which we speak is beyond words and any mental conceptualization. This Love, which we can also call "God" (or Source, Spirit, Oneness, etc) is really the place we return to when we let go of everything that is not of Love. Otherwise put, it is what we realize we are when the ego is completely dissolved. So why use words at all to talk about it? While this is indeed a valid question and point, the book is for those who still might find useful in clarifying what is egoic and what is not. In other words, what is of Love, and what is not of Love. This is not always so easy to discern!

The third offering in the series is also unique in that it is a "family affair" -- it is not the work of Allowah alone, but is also by his wife, Beata, and their baby, Sonny. One nice feature of the book is not only the beautiful family pictures included, but the way in which the love of one small family can be seen to reflect the Universal Love that we really are all seeking.

We feel that these 3 books, this trilogy, offers great insight into the human condition and how we might rise beyond our limited, egoic conditioning and realize our True Divine Nature at last. While perhaps no book could ever actually lead to a state of permanent enlightenment (& we don't rule out the possibility), there are books that can and do serve as portals and pointers toward a Reality that is beyond all words and concepts. We believe that the books in the Who Am I? series, if read carefully, can certainly serve in such a capacity and be "truly helpful" to all sincere seekers of truth.

WHO AM I?

YOGA, PSYCHEDELICS AND THE QUEST FOR ENLIGHTENMENT

ALLOWAH LANI

Receiving the blessing on my first book by my guru & favorite yoga teacher,
Sri Dharma Mittra, Friend of the Dharma,
Sun of Righteousness.

ALLOWAH LANI

I AM LOVE
Nothing Happened

**YOGA
AYAHUASCA
A COURSE IN MIRACLES**
*And The Journey Back
To The Place We Never Left*

Love is

The eternal way to true happiness

By Allowah & Beata Lani

THAT THOU ART

Classic Source Texts for the Study, Practice and Experience of Advaita Vedanta

ALLOWAH LANI

Heart 'n' Hands

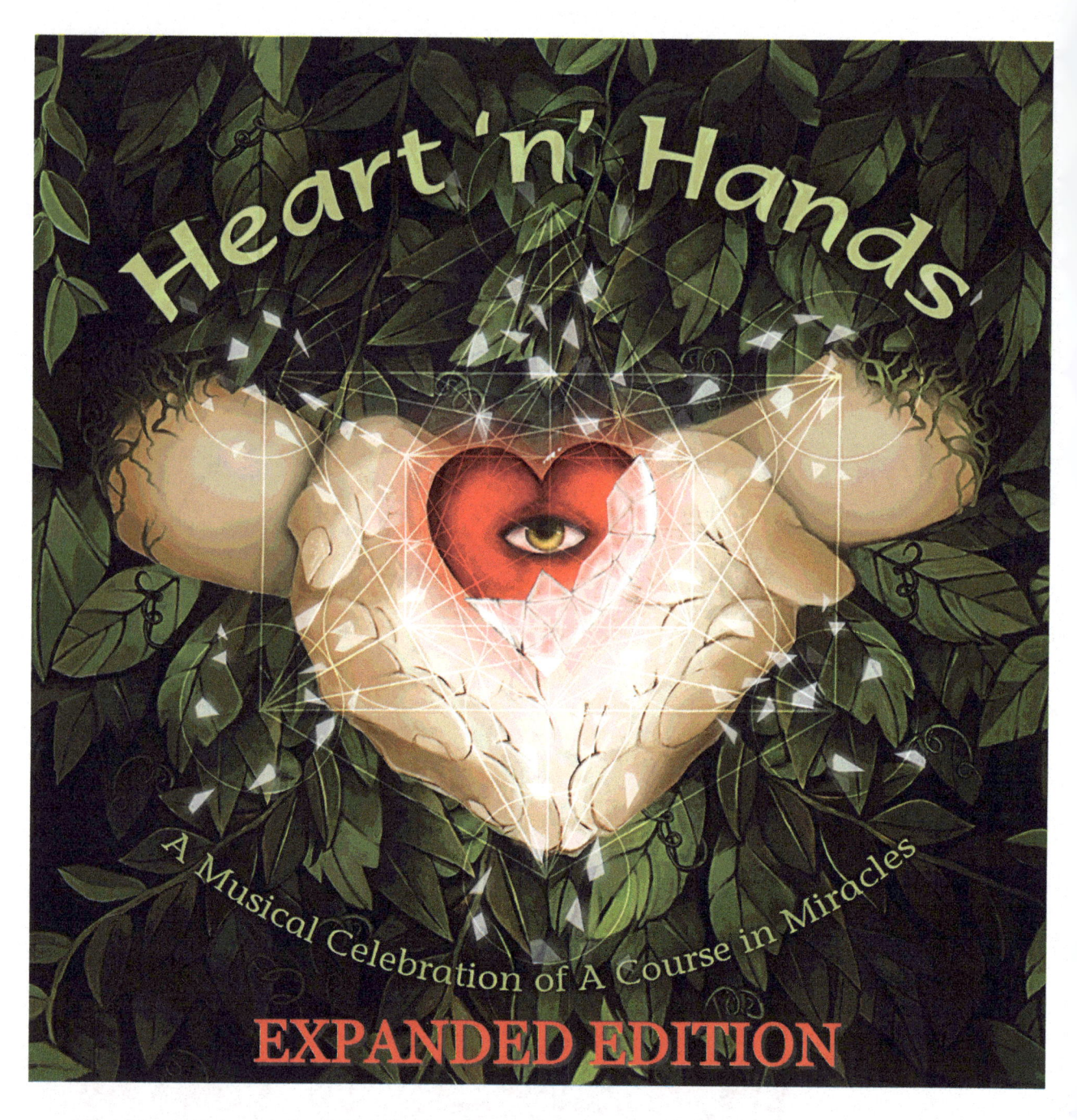

A Musical Celebration of A Course in Miracles

EXPANDED EDITION

This is an entire double album of music inspired by *A Course in Miracles*.

One disc contains the studio versions of the songs, and the other disc contains live versions of most of the songs from a performance at the Unity Church in Naples, Florida.

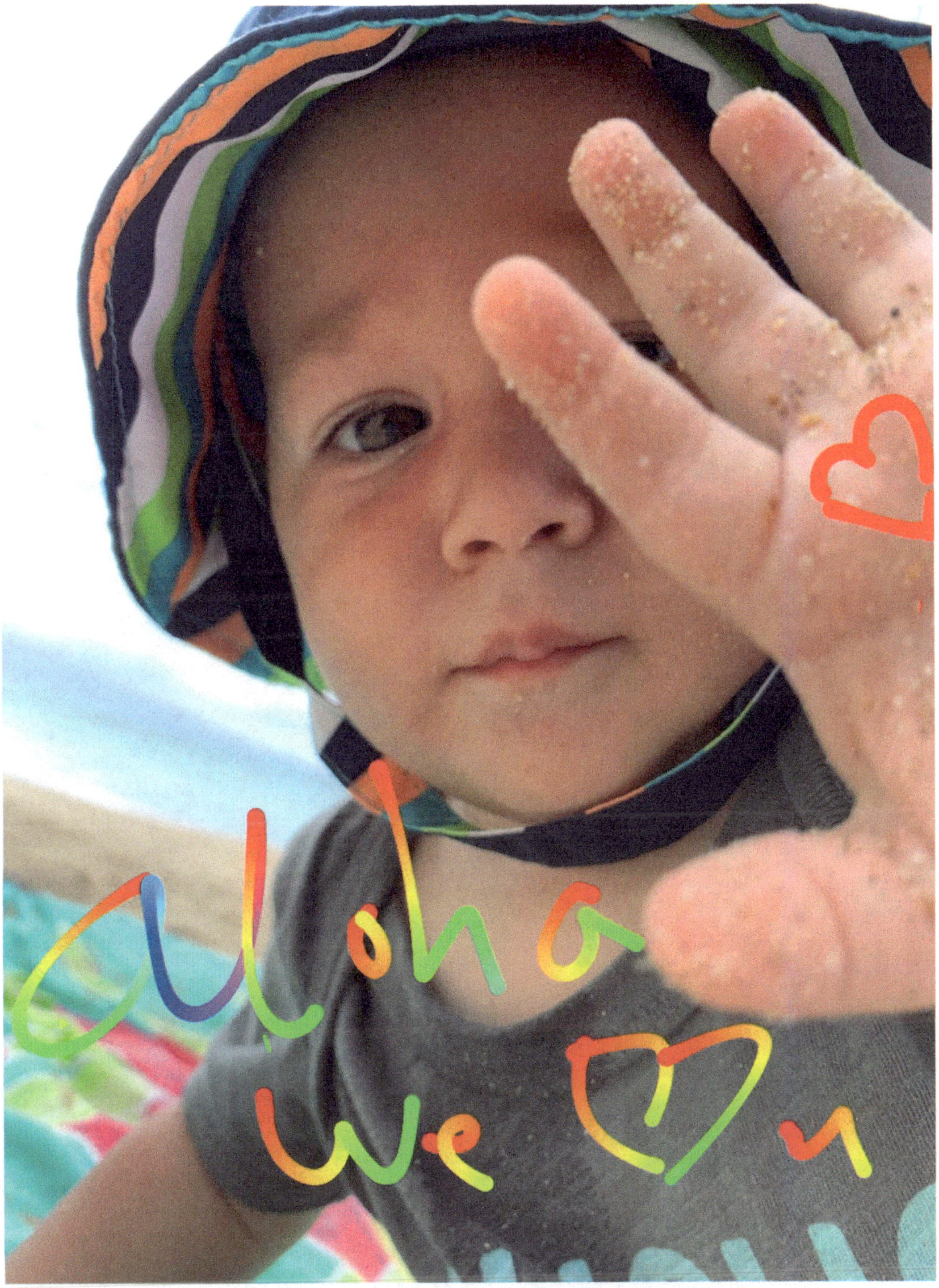
aloha
We ♡ u

Forever

How to Connect With Us...

Cell: (239) 592-0898

Email: allowah13@gmail.com

FB: Truly Helpful

IG: Truly Helpful

Website: www.trulyhelpful.love